CW01150246

SUCCESS & PROSPERITY

INSIGHTS FROM THE BOOK
"WHAT MAKES OUR LIFE A SUCCESS"

MORDECHAI AND ESTHER FINTZ

Copyright © 2024 Mordechai and Esther Fintz.

All rights reserved. No part of this book may be reproduced, stored, or transmitted by any means—whether auditory, graphic, mechanical, or electronic—without written permission of both publisher and author, except in the case of brief excerpts used in critical articles and reviews. Unauthorized reproduction of any part of this work is illegal and is punishable by law.

This is a work of nonfiction.

ISBN: 979-8-89419-533-9 (sc)
ISBN: 979-8-89419-534-6 (hc)
ISBN: 979-8-89419-535-3 (e)

Because of the dynamic nature of the Internet, any web addresses or links contained in this book may have changed since publication and may no longer be valid. The views expressed in this work are solely those of the author and do not necessarily reflect the views of the publisher, and the publisher hereby disclaims any responsibility for them.

THE EWINGS PUBLISHING

One Galleria Blvd., Suite 1900, Metairie, LA 70001
(504) 702-6708

The Illustrated Torah Scroll

TO

MORDECHAI AND ESTHER

MAZEL TOV AND SUCCESS

ON YOUR NEW BOOK

"WHAT MAKES OUR LIFE A SUCCESS"

Amen

Paintings by Michal Meron

Copyrights © by The Studio in Old Jaffa

All rights reserved. No part of this publication may be reproduced or transmitted in any form or by any means, electronic or mechanical including photocopying, recording or any information storage and retrieval system, without prior permission in writing from the publishers.

DISCLAIMER:

The authors wish to emphasize that they do not, in any way, hold themselves out as licensed marriage counselors. Although they are available for marriage encounter sessions or to offer advice solely **based on personal experience**, they do not act in the capacity of legal counselors, mediators, therapists, social workers, or other licensed professionals.

To schedule a marriage encounter session at your place of business or worship, please direct your inquiry to mordechai@makelifeasuccess.com

Visit us on Facebook, Instagram, Youtube, and at our website: makelifeasuccess.com

ABOUT OUR LOGO

The two circles represent the ring we continue to wear proudly since the day we took our vows. The circle signifies our love's unending wholeness. When God unified our lives, that commitment was meant to last on earth into eternity. The two flamingos in the center represent us, forming a heart that unifies us inside our Circle of Love, surrounded by the Circle of Life. They also symbolize our connection and union of two hearts as *one*, enabling us to make our life a success.

CONTENTS

Readers' Commentaries xi
Dedication xvii
Acknowledgments xix
About the Authors xxv
Preface xxix

Chapter 1 What Faith in God Means to Us 1
There Are Two Levels of Faith In God 8
Lessons In Faith and God-given Destiny 16

**Chapter 2 A Testimony of Obedience that
                      Turned Into a Forever Love** 19
Trusting In God to Find Our Soul Mate 35

Chapter 3 What Makes a Marriage Successful? 41
The Benefits of Finding Our Soul mate 41
Pray and Trust in God 44
Our Sleeping Habits 48
Our Food Preferences 49
Our Place of Worship, Family Meetings, and
   Our Children's Religious Upbringing 50
Religious Education and Practices 52
Place of Residence 53
Follow the Principle of One Family 53
Never Go to Sleep Angry 54
Never Speak Negatively About Your Mate 55
It's About "WE," NOT "I" 57
Mutually Agree on Financial Matters 58
Intimacy Is Not Just Physical; It Is An Expression of
   Love At All Times 61

A UNION OF HEARTS SHOULD ENDURE DURING OUR
TEMPORAL LIVES INTO ETERNITY

CONTENTS, CONTINUED

Create Lasting Memories 65
Balance Your Spiritual Income and Expenditures
    On Your Life's Balance Sheet 67
To Say "I Love You" 76

Chapter 4 Doing it God's Way 77
The Two-Dollar Certificate 83
The Dollar Torah 85
The AY-YA-YA-YA-YAI Cheer 86
Lessons to Treasure from "Doing It God's Way" 89

Chapter 5 Decision-Making Through Divine Consultation 91
Lessons of the Heart: Consulting God to Help Us
    Make Proper Decisions 97
Affirmations to Help Us Maintain God In the
    Decision-Making Process 98

Chapter 6 Angels in Our Midst 99
Our Granddaughter's Encounter With An Angel 106
How Do We Become Angels In This World? 109
Lessons in Encountering Angels 110
A Personal Testimony About the Angel In China 112
Affirmation to Become Part of God's Angelic Army...................115

Chapter 7 The Reasons We Should Not Ask God "Why?" 117
Are You Mentally Wavering Between Doubt and Faith? 121
Mourning Our Relatives When They Pass On is a
    Gift From God 122
Should We Question God's Reasons For Taking Those
    Whom We Love and Care About Before Their Time? 124
Why Do We Mentally Wrestle with Ourselves When
    Making Decisions? 127

COMPROMISE IN THE MARITAL RELATIONSHIP—AS IN ALL INSTANCES—IS CRUCIAL TO A HEALTHY, LASTING CONNECTION

CONTENTS, CONTINUED

Has God Provided Us with Instructions on How to Live? 128
When Destruction and Suffering Occur,
    How Should People React? 129
Understanding Our Purpose 131
Lessons in Recognizing the Presence of God 134
Prayer for Turning Whys Into Faith 136

Chapter 8 Tests of Our Faith **137**
How Tests of Faith Have Led Us to the Blessings of
    Success and Spiritual Growth 138
The Lessons In Our Tests 145
Lessons In Endurance 146
Prayer of Faith 147

Chapter 9 From a Celebration to a Test,
    From Tribulation to Victory **149**
Lessons In Overcoming Challenges and Encountering
    a Higher Purpose 162

Chapter 10 The Love of God Inspires Us to Love Others **165**

Concluding Thoughts From "Mr. Amen" 171
List of Quotations 177

TRUST IN THE CREATOR IS THE SPARK THAT IGNITES
AND MANIFESTS OUR DREAMS

READERS' COMMENTARIES

First Edition

Some of our readers graciously bestowed the following commentaries after the publication of this book's first edition. We are most grateful for their support and appreciation.

Jason—New York

I had such an inspirational experience reading your book. Your quotes and thoughts are full of wisdom and the enlight-enment you have received from God. It was also a pleasure to read about your personal experiences and love for one another, family, and God, as well as the immense strength you receive in faith. Your words have increased my own faith.

There were a few passages that I took special note of that resonated with me and I want to call upon when needed:

"God has a purpose and a reason for everything. Tests are the building blocks of victory."

"Not everything goes right all the time. When things do not turn out according to our expectations, we have complete faith that everything will work for the best."

"God, like a teacher, presents tests to see if we have learned our lessons." (This came from Aunt Raquel.)

"Faith is like an electric plug: we can be connected to God or be unplugged and use our own energy. When we are not plugged into the power that created us, we will eventually run out of energy."

You also said that "every time you give with honorable intention, you receive much more because you are doing God's work." You will be giving enrichment to each and every indi-vidual who reads your book, and sharing how proper applica-tions of faith and love intertwine to bring success to our lives and is an amazing way of doing God's work. May you receive good fortune from the beautiful book you authored.

Rachel-North Bay Village, FL

This book is a "must read" by all who question "why" and "why me." It teaches us, through the authors' own experiences, that instead of asking "why," we say that God must have a reason for the things that happen in our life, and through those expe-riences, we learn how to first be grateful. Secondly, we must accept the lessons we learn from those experiences that we face each day through our life. Throughout the book, we learn that success is not only a physical achievement, but it is a spiritual one, as well. We reach that final success when we become one with the Eternal Light. AMEN.

Michelle–Hollywood

Mordechai and Esther, the authors of this book, attach their daily actions and attitude to their words. Yes, sometimes life throws us lemons and making lemonade is the most profound lesson we learn from those experiences. This is the Fintz recipe for making that (flavor of) lemonade! Even if your lemonade is a bit sour at first, their positive energy and strong faith will inspire and encourage any reader to keep adding the sugar to make life sweeter!

Josie-Texas

I loved and enjoyed reading, What makes Our Life A Success? It is all so meaningful to me, but the one chapter that meant the most to me is, "Angels In Our Midst."

I personally went through a very difficult and traumatizing few years of my life and I felt that G-d was with me all through it, giving me strength to survive. Just like it is written in the book, I too felt the presence of our almighty G-d guiding me, and sometimes using people as Angels to help me all through it, and if it were not for my faith in G-d and His help I would not have survived.

Nobody can deny that we all go through difficult test in our lives, especially when we are going through a hard and dark path. Keeping the faith in G- d, we find that the Almighty is, helping us fight our battles. I felt the more faith that I had in G-d, the more things turned around in a positive way. I learned that if I keep my faith in G-d, no matter how bad things are, G-d will make all things possible for us in positive ways.

G -d also brings people into our lives, as Angels and messen-gers from G-d, to guide and help us through hard times, and to strengthen us, when we need them the most.

I congratulate Mordechai and Esther for writing this mean-ingful, healing, inspiring and wonderful book that I will keep for years to come. I will read it very often and will recommend it to anyone that I know.

Joanne and Irving Shulkes

Dear Esther and Mordechai,

In the book, What Makes Our Life a Success?", we find answers to the perplexing questions and inevitable challenges of daily living. Whether looking for a wife or wrestling with a financial reversal, there is a path to follow. God is the guiding light and the omnipresent force. We can feel the abiding faith and optimism of Esther and Mordechai Fintz on every page.

One's way of life, their beliefs, should be governed by kindness, compassion and caring. Of course, we might be able to accomplish these things on our own.

It is when we partner with God, however, that we can live our lives with greater dignity and meaning. Esther and Mordechai take us from where we are to where we ought to be. Surely, all of us know how difficult this path can be.

We heartily recommend this book.

With love,

Irving and Joanne

Bonnie-Hollywood

When I read this book, I was on an airplane with a feeling of being close to heaven. I was incredibly moved by the faith and love that Mordechai and Esther have for life and each other. I thought people who do not know them may wonder – are they for real? I can tell you that they have been my friends for 30 years and they are the real deal! A couple committed to each other and wanting to share their faith and love with humanity. I am truly blessed that they in are in my life.

AMEN!

Diego–Fort Lauderdale

For many, this book will be candid, interesting, eye-opening and easy to digest. For me, it was all those things and more. From the beginning, it ignited in me the flame of curiosity. During my journey through the book, I felt as if I was traveling alongside the authors through the journey of their lives. I wanted to learn more, understand more, and know more. The authors' teachings are easy to grasp and straightforward in their presen-tation, and do not attempt to impose a belief on the readers. There is a saying that goes: "you can bring a horse to the river, but you cannot make it drink." This book is about the authors bringing the readers to the river, not making them drink. It is up to each reader to drink from the river of love, admire it as it flows downstream, or simply walk away. The most important thing to remember about this book is that the authors do not intend to change anyone's beliefs. They simply want to share their knowledge and show the readers that anything is possible if they act with love, kindness and faith.

Lina and Israel
(Mordechai's Parents)

Lea and Leon Behar
(Esther's Parents)

DEDICATION

*To My Beloved Aunt Raquel and Mother Lina—
my guiding lights and spiritual advisors.*

*L: Raquel Cordovi Rodriguez (July 1, 1924-December 11, 2011)
R: Lina Fintz (February 20, 1922-January 18, 2010)*

Sarita Rosenwald, Esther's Aunt

ACKNOWLEDGMENTS

Esther and I wish to thank **GOD, THE ETERNAL SOURCE**, for illuminating and guiding us. Every word of this text was inspired by God through prayerful reflection.

To ***our granddaughter, Sara, and our granddaughter, Mindy, and her husband, Carlos,*** for providing inspiration and encour-agement in this endeavor.

To ***our sister, Rachel, and late brother-in-law, Sal,*** we express our most profound gratitude for their support and encourage-ment throughout the process of writing and publication.

To ***our son, Izzy, and our daughter-in-law, Janice****,* we wish to acknowledge their support and encouragement in writing this book.

Cantor Irving and Joanne Shulkes have our love and appreciation for their insightful perspectives regarding this writing, along with

Michelle and Marv Henderson and Sharon Molot for their unwavering inspiration and support.

- xx -

ACKNOWLEDGMENTS, CONTINUED

To our dear friend, renowned Israeli artist, **Michal Meron**, for his gift of the illustrated Torah, a special dedication and blessing upon this book.

To **Cantor Norman Cohen Falah** of Temple Sinai of North Dade, musician, composer, and chorus director, our deepest gratitude flows for your creative lyrical compositions.

"Flamingos" by Carlos Rodriguez

A painting dedicated to the authors to commemorate their trip to Israel. The Flamingos represent the authors, backdropped by buildings and the Dome of the Rock Shrine, the camel is a reminder of their memorable ride, the canoes memorialize their passage through the Jordan River, flowing roughly north, through the Sea of Galilee, and the swirling stars in the heavens represent their beloved departed, watching over them.

ACKNOWLEDGMENTS, CONTINUED

To the Ewings Publishing Team and our Editor, Gabriella, our heartfelt thanks for your collaboration in bringing our vision to life. Your efforts have made our book cover design truly perfect, and we deeply appreciate your dedication and creativity.

We wish to express our sincere gratitude to **Austin Lias,** a renowned Cuban editor and publisher, who guided our efforts from the beginning of this journey and encouraged us to write this book.

To our writing collaborator, **Gabriella Gafni**, we extend our thanks for expressing our message from the heart, in simple prose, and for sharing positive and inspiring thoughts with per-sistence and dedication.

To **our "committee" of friends** who took time to carefully evaluate this book and provide feedback, we thank you.

And to many others—far too numerous to list here—our appreciation has no bounds.

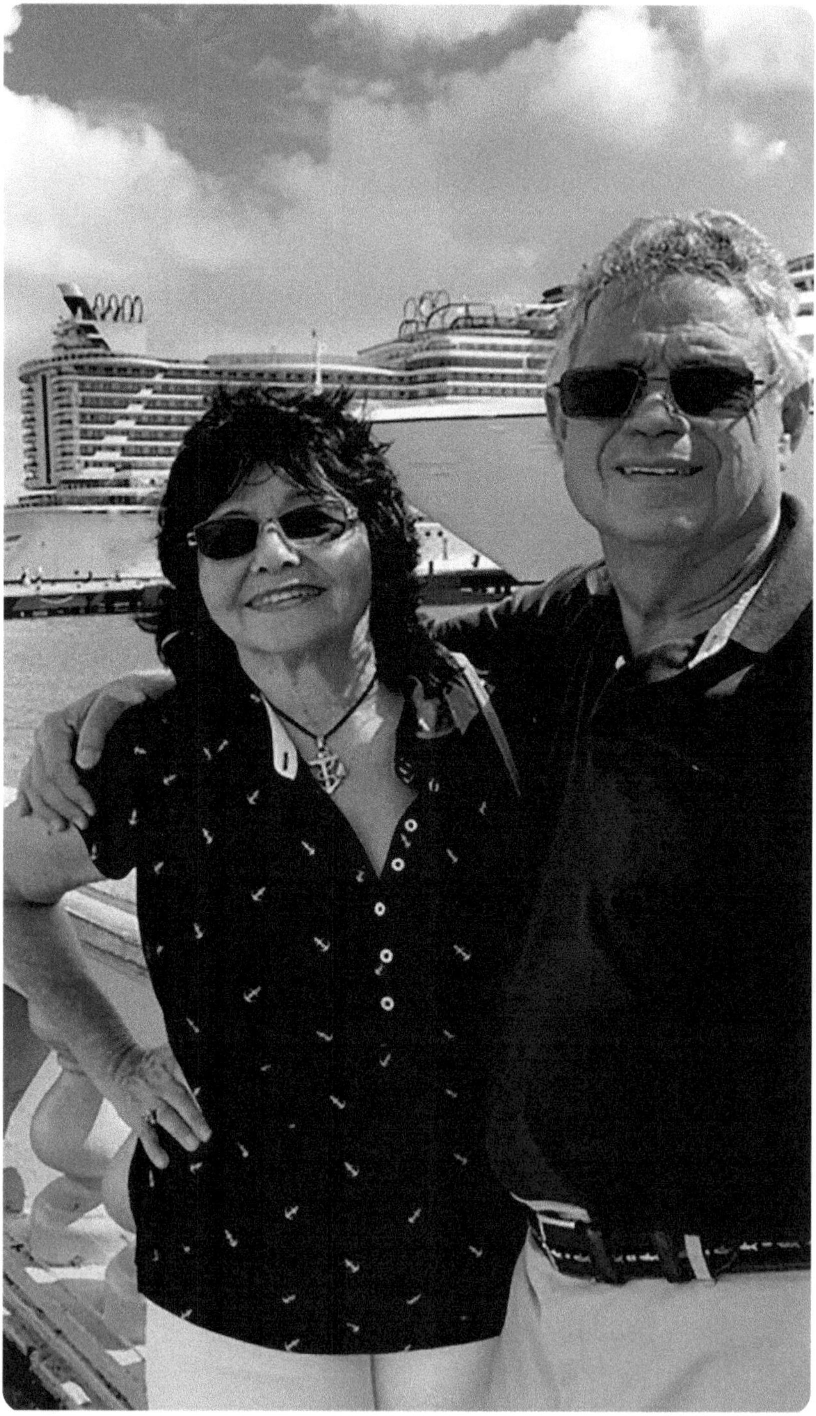

ABOUT THE AUTHORS

Marcos ("Mordechai") Fintz, the youngest of four children, was born in Cuba in 1945. His ancestors came from Turkey. In 1961, fourteen- year-old Esther left Cuba for Jamaica, where she and her family stayed until they obtained the necessary docu-mentation to travel to the United States. It took great courage for both families to leave the comfort and familiarity of their homes and embark on an entirely new adventure in an unknown land, but apparently, God orchestrated Esther and Mordechai's meeting in New York one year later, merging two lives of similar backgrounds and ancestral histories).

The immigration process hardly seemed like a bright prospect for the authors, then barely into their teens, but as with every other endeavor or challenge in their lives, they placed their faith wholeheartedly in God as their ultimate source of abundance.

To help his family make ends meet, Mordechai worked in construction as a bricklayer and wall finisher in Israel. A year later, his Aunt Raquel, a very influential figure in his life with enormous spiritual gifts, encouraged the family to settle in the United States. Later, after the family arrived in America, she helped Mordechai to grow spiritually. Eventually, under her guidance, Mordechai found his soul mate, Esther (whom he met in Brooklyn, New York) . It is ironic (not to mention an act of divine intervention) that the couple had similar backgrounds, came from the same region, and traveled a long distance under the same circumstances to find one another thousands of miles away from home.

Aunt Raquel continued to instruct Mordechai in the ways of faith and encouraged him to maintain a positive outlook, even in the face of challenges and hardships.

**May the reflection of each sunrise
and sunset illuminate your soul.
Amen.**

Through faith in God and family guidance, the young couple learned to honor and praise God for prosperity in their lives. They also practiced courage and perseverance in times of strife. With Aunt Raquel's assistance, they learned patience and the importance of gratitude, faith, inner strength, and character-building. With this solid foundation, the couple began a family of their own. Their first-born son, Israel, named after his paternal grandfather, was the light of their lives and the beacon of a new generation.

Faith always has been the cornerstone of the authors' lives and has inspired them to share their perspectives with others. In these pages, you will find inspiring, uplifting stories that Mordechai and Esther learned throughout their lives together. Also, the authors share lessons they have learned from reading and listening to the teachings of many professionals and religious leaders. They hope their readers will begin to experience and live a life of faith, love, success, abundance, spiritual growth, peace, and happiness.

God inspired the authors to impart these teachings, practices, and experiences with the hope that their readers will reap sig-nificant benefits, just as they have. The text is written in plain, practical, understandable language to appeal to a mass audience.

Mordechai and Esther want to emphasize that they do not intend to promote or endorse any one religion or belief over another. While sharing their deeply personal views, they adopt an open-hearted, universal approach to subjects, stories, and events that are dear to their hearts.

**May you soar on wings of faith with a firm
belief that all you will manifest in God's time.**

PREFACE

This book aims to share our knowledge and understanding of how we can be successful in all aspects of our lives. Abundance occurs as we grow and embark on our spiritual journey—no matter where we are in our lives, the religion we practice, or the house of worship we attend. This book will help readers expand their knowledge and provide a new perspective for them to consider. We will also discuss our true purpose in life and what makes our life a success.

God's wisdom has inspired us throughout our lifetimes. We have also learned from various teachers whom we have been privileged to encounter and from books, seminars, and meditation. We hope, therefore, to present our views and the lessons that God has placed in our path to enhance our life experiences through different tests. As a result, God has allowed us to see and feel divine mercy, understand life, and the fact that God has prepared us for the final success—eternal life. Each chapter will take the readers into various aspects of life's trajectory and inspire them to explore enlightening, life-affirming topics that will lead to a more fulfilling, joyful, and inspiring existence.

Since this text's first edition was published, we have expanded our reach by offering marriage encounter sessions. Although we do not hold ourselves out as marriage counselors, our decades-long union has served as an example to countless couples.

It is important to note that this book does not endorse any specific organized religion or belief system. We believe God, as worshipped in every religion, is the same God that created the universe—the water and the earth—humankind, every plant, animal, and living being.

We offer a faith-based, non-demoninational approach. We perceive God as gender-neutral—the universal life-force energy that creates and directs all living things in our universe. As such, we refer to God only by that name, without a gender designa-tion. We also spell the full name, GOD, without abbreviations.

In the Jewish faith, we traditionally write the word G-D. However, we prayed and thought about the matter and maintained the conviction that we must spell the entire name GOD, even though different religions refer to the Holy Name in various ways.

A note about the narration/voice also bears mention here. After the Introduction, the body of the text will be in Mordechai's first-person narrative. However, each viewpoint and message also expresses Esther's approach and philosophical perspective.

As to the views expressed here, particularly about an afterlife, we know that every religion expresses its own viewpoint, and each interpretation is different. At the same time, every religion points to the same Creator. We always hear people say, "How can I believe in an afterlife when no one has returned from the other side to tell us all about it?" Well, that is an opinion that most people in this world will adopt right away, even though deep inside, they believe there is more to living than just life, death, and burial.

We have found that the conversation goes sour whenever we speak with someone about preparing the soul or spirit for a meeting with our Creator. Nearly everyone believes this subject is taboo and depressing, and just thinking or talking about it will take away the joy, success, and fun in life.

We are writing this book to demonstrate that this perception is erroneous. The reverse is true. Immersing oneself in spirituality and knowing what awaits us in the afterlife, "on the other side," increases our sense of individual empowerment, enlightenment, and purpose. It removes all our fears and provides us with the God-given power to accomplish success in all aspects of our lives, including our health.

Once we understand why God has created us and what we are made of, we will realize how ultimate "success" is defined and how we can enjoy life on earth to the fullest while knowing that eternal joy awaits us.

Undoubtedly, readers will have their own views on the subjects we address, and we sincerely respect differences of opinion. We pray to God that in learning about our views, our readers will sense our sincerity and receive our perspectives in the way they are offered—with love, respect, solidarity, good faith, and hope.

These roses are symbols of love. The authors dedicate them to their parents and Tía Sarita Rosenwald, who are rejoicing in the eternal peace of God.

**Faith is a butterfly who once was a caterpillar
that never stopped believing.**

CHAPTER 1

WHAT FAITH IN GOD MEANS TO US

When referring to faith in God, my wife Esther and I want to emphasize that we place exclusive, unconditional faith in the Source with the complete acceptance that God is the Creator of the entire universe. We firmly believe that God created human beings to have various skin colors, speak different languages, be born in different countries, have diverse ways of worshiping, and engage in diverse cultural and spiritual practices. That is all part of God's plan. Most significantly, our souls do not have a color, characteristic, or manner of glorifying God.

1
THE ENERGY OF OUR SOUL DOES NOT HAVE A COLOR OR A GENDER. IT IS PART OF THE ENERGY OF GOD

There is only one Creator of the world and the universe, and even though there are different races, creeds, and colors, all of us have the same quest to love and respect one another and serve God, regardless of our Circle of Love, country of origin, or spoken language. In our own ways, wherever we are, we must demonstrate faith in God—through action—by loving one another and accepting our differences.

One of our most important missions is to love and respect all the humans in this world, no matter how different they may be from us or how they worship God. We should not judge others. Only the Creator, our God, will judge each one of us, and that judgment is based on how we interact, believe, correct our mistakes, and look for ways to bring words and acts of kindness to everyone around us. We should not discriminate against anyone or reject others because of how they believe and worship God. Instead, we must think of faith in God as the common thread unifying us all.

2
WE MUST THINK OF FAITH IN GOD AS THE COMMON THREAD THAT UNIFIES ALL OF US

God is the Divine Source that gives us the strength and confidence to believe in ourselves and helps us acquire the requisite knowledge of our life's mission and how to actualize it. Faith in God helps us in every difficult circumstance, such as illnesses, disappointments, and life's innumerable challeng-es and hardships. Through faith, the Almighty places the right people in our path to facilitate our goals, achieve success, and complete our mission—whether that means finding the ap-propriate doctor or medication to treat particular illnesses or finding connections in our workplace, career, family, or other relationships.

Outcomes are entirely dependent on God's will.

Our lives are filled with many testimonies of faith. I will try to share a few in the pages of this book. I realize that they may not be very significant to you, but to us, big or small, they have profound meaning, and each one has helped us grow in faith—one step at a time. We could see God's presence in every testimony we presented, and we hope they will inspire you.

If you believe everything is possible, you will achieve victory by believing and inviting God into everything you do. When you present your desires and goals to God, the Creator will help you to achieve your goal and complete your mission. The following story illustrates this point.

3
IF YOU BELIEVE, ALL THINGS ARE POSIBLE. IT ALL STARTS BY INVITING GOD INTO YOUR LIFE

We had just moved to Florida from New York with our son, Izzy, who was one year old. We rented a furnished apartment on the beach to be closer to my in-laws, and I was offered a job as a manager in a bathing suit manufacturing company in Hialeah, Florida.

I had just turned twenty, and Esther was eighteen. The factory had many sewing operators, and my job was to supervise the pro-duction, improve the quality of the garments, and increase pro-duction. The owner provided me with a fixed base salary with a nice incentive bonus, intending to produce a certain number of garments monthly. The amount he gave me was unattainable for past managers. He told me I would earn $0.50 for every garment produced over that amount in a month.

Here was how God's blessings took shape. We prayed and asked the Source to help and provide us with ideas and methods to simultaneously increase production and maintain excellent quality. During the first few days, I observed each operator and came to understand how they viewed the garments. The process was complex because I was very young, and, in their eyes, I did not have the knowledge or expertise to manage them. However, I always felt that God was helping and assuring me I had what it took to do the job and that the Creator would ensure my ability to assist. I knew that God had a purpose for our life.

The owner never told the operators that I spoke Spanish, and as I walked down the aisle to inspect the quality and oversaw what they were sewing, they usually made ridiculous, degrading comments. However, I didn't pay attention.

After a few days of observation, God gave me an idea about how to increase production and improve the quality of the garments. With that in mind, I asked to meet with the owner, who agreed to see me in his office at 4:00 p.m. after work. When I arrived at his office, his son was there to participate in our meeting. I told him that God had shown me the way to increase productivity and, at the same time, improve the garment's quality. The owner encouraged me to speak my mind, but his son gave me a very negative look, as if to say, you will not be able to succeed; but I always placed my trust in and concentra-tion on God, the provider of all things. I presented the plan and what I needed to make it work.

4
MY TRUST AND CONCENTRATION ARE ALWAYS FOCUSED ON GOD, THE PROVIDER OF ALL THINGS

"We are going to implement a system of section piecework, and instead of paying the operators by the hour as we were paying them, you will have a fixed cost for each garment. I will divide the assembly of the garments into several sections, with each operator specializing in a different section. That way, we will have better quality garments, and, at the same time, pro-duction will increase by allowing the operators to make more money. Therefore, they will be happier at work."

Even though he could not understand everything I proposed, the owner was pleased with my presentation and liked the idea of having a fixed cost for the garments. He approved me to move forward with the plan and agreed to provide me with everything I needed because he wanted to improve production and quality.

My wife and I thanked God in advance for giving us the victory. The following week, we started with a different approach. My first order of business to gain respect was to approach the Spanish-speaking operators who were always making rash comments about me. I said in Spanish, "Please can you allow me to show you how to sew that garment better and faster? The person that I addressed (a female) began to cry, stood up, and asked for forgiveness, assuring me that she did not know I spoke Spanish.

SUCCESS & PROSPERITY

I said, "Apology accepted, and please forgive me because I should have told everyone on the first day I came here."

I sat down and showed her how to set up the garment sections and save time, and I began to sow quickly. Everyone stopped what they were doing to watch what was going on. I took that opportunity to explain the changes that would soon take place and, as a result, how everyone s would benefit. "Instead of getting paid by the hour, you will be paid by the pieces, and the garment will be done on section piece work," I explained.

The following week, we were presented with challenges, and, like everything else in life, people do not always welcome change. It often brings fear and worry, but I had patience, per-sistence, perseverance, and, most significantly, faith in God. I went from machine to machine, giving each operator confidence and ways to work faster and better. One by one, as the day pro-gressed, they were able to rise to the challenges and saw that they were making more money. The process was much easier, and the quality improved one hundred percent due to the repetitive work. That week, the owner's son told me the plan would not work and that I would fail. I replied, "With all due respect, your comments are useless because I listen to and obey God."

We learned that life is filled with trials and tribulations. When God allows stumbling blocks and negative people try to control and convince us that we will fail, we must maintain faith in God and remember that everything that happens in our life is part of the divine plan to help us grow in faith.

5
GOD ALLOWS STUMBLING BLOCKS AND NEGATIVE PEOPLE TO TEST AND PROVIDE US WITH THE TOOLS OF FAITH TO HAVE VICTORY AND MOVE US TO THE NEXT LEVEL

The following Monday, the factory's atmosphere and positive energy were at a height. We ended the month, surpass-ing the goal only by a few hundred garments, but that was a very positive outcome. The following month we practically doubled production, and the quality was excellent. The factory did not receive any returned merchandise from the new production. The operators were making more money than they had ever dreamed of, and the owner was delighted to witness the vast improve-ments in productivity and quality. He came to congratulate the entire group of factory employees and me. I thanked everyone present and gave God the honor and glory. For some reason, the only unhappy person was the owner's son; but that didn't matter to me. I had God on my side.

The following month God made us even more successful. My bonus was double the salary that the owner was paying me. As a result, his son became even more verbally combative, and the owner did not want to pay my bonus the following month. At that time, we decided that we had to take different paths, and I understood that everything was happening according to God's plan.

With the help of our Uncle Enrique, we opened our wholesale distribution center, leading us to the creation of "Lina's Fashions," a family-owned business.

The story's moral: We had to go through the hardship of challenges before emerging into the light of our potential and following the plan God designed for us. .

There Are Two Levels of Faith In God

Level One consists of those souls who have faith, are obedient to God, and believe that everything in their lives is happening for their best. The individuals who have achieved this level of faith will find peace, consolation, success, and prosperity. We can have a better attitude and outlook on life with faith and belief that God is working for our best. Our goals, missions, health challenges, financial issues, family matters, and other preoccu-pations will transform into victories because we no longer allow our minds to wander or worry. Our trust and love for God will increase. At that point, we will be ready to grow into the second level of faith.

Level Two is more advanced and requires more commitment and a firm belief that God has a reason and purpose for our good in every circumstance in our lives. God is continuously testing us. The purpose of the tests that human beings experience is to help us grow more in this world, achieve all our dreams and goals, complete our missions, and attain the highest level of spirituality in the world to come. This level of faith requires a complete submission of our will to God. However, this does not mean that we become robots. God will give us ideas, the correct person, and the most beneficial opportunities to achieve our goals. At the same time, we must be able to use everything God gives us—along with faith and perseverance— to attain our advancement in faith and progress on our journey in this world. When we achieve this degree of faith, God will allow our intellect to be in constant communication with the Master of the Universe, and we will be able to confront all the chal-lenges before us, knowing that God has a plan for everything happening in our lives. With that faith in God, we will always see the victories, go from strength to strength, and ultimately triumph. At the same time, we will have the satisfaction of rec-ognizing that whatever is happening in our lives is for the best and God has a definite purpose.

In the presence of faith, all darkness, fear, stress, and doubt disappear. With faith in God, we are ensured the proper guidance and direction we require in every aspect of our daily lives. Throughout all the tests and tribulations that we have gone through over the years and continue to experience, we have been very privileged and blessed to grow more in faith. When we live a life of faith, we reflect its light for all to witness—whomever we encounter. Everyone surrounding us will be able to see that all that occurs in our lives is taking place for our good through faith in God, who provides the victory to those who patiently wait for divine mercy.

6
GOD PROVIDES THE VICTORY TO THOSE WHO PATIENTLY WAIT FOR DIVINE MERCY

Consider incorporating the following affirmations into your life. Declare the following, believing with all your heart and spirit:

I WANT TO GROW MY FAITH IN GOD

(1) When I open my eyes in the morning, I will show my gratitude to God for this day, and I will see that God's creation is made of perfect balance in this world.
(2) I will accept that God is always working in my life for my best.
(3) I will accept that God has a plan and a purpose for me today.
(4) I will look for ideas, signs, and opportunities that God will provide through my inner voice and through the signs that appear around me.
(5) I will always count my blessings for all the things that God continues to provide.
(6) I will accept the fact that having faith in God means that I will believe in the things that will come, and that faith will allow the outcome to rest on God's time and not mine.
(7) I will always count my blessings and start each day by giving thanks to God.
(8) I will believe that God will help me to reach my goals and complete my mission at the correct time.
(9) I will rest on the wisdom of God, and each day will be a blessing for me no matter what may be happening in my life.
(10) Several times a day, I will silently repeat that God is my source, my shield and my salvation, the provider of everything. And whatever will be happening today, whether I think that it is good or is bad, I will know that it is for my best.

Amen.

I will read these affirmations each day, absorb and practice them, and I will see the difference in my life and the prosperity, peace, and happiness my family and I will experience.

7
GOD IS THE PROVIDER OF EVERYTHING.
GOD WILL BE WITH ME ALL THE DAYS OF MY LIFE.
I WILL TRY MY BEST, WITH PERSISTENCE AND FAITH, AND GOD WILL DO THE REST

The following additional personal testimony is a prime example of faith in action in our lives.

Some years ago, we resolved a matter that perfectly illus-trates our point of what it means to have faith in God, rest on God's time, be persistent, and witness a successful outcome. Please know that I am not recounting this story to impress our readers with our faith but rather, to impress *upon* you that faith in God is the sole resource we need to succeed in this life, no matter what trials we must endure.

For the last few years, we have been facing many financial challenges, and we have had to communicate and deal with experts and bankers to refinance one of our properties. To observers who witness our challenges, the following question sometimes arises: "If you have so much faith in God, why are there so many obstacles associated with finding the right bank for your purposes?"

We always reply: "We will trust in God, who has a purpose for everything and guides us toward the best outcomes in every respect."

8
GOD IS ALWAYS WORKING FOR OUR BENEFIT, EVEN IN THE MIDST OF THE GREATEST TRIALS

The following is another true personal account. Every day, we place our faith in God during morning prayers. As part of my ritual, I put on the tefillin (cubic black leather boxes with leather straps that Jewish men wear on their heads and arms during weekday morning prayer). After completing the tefillin prayers, we add affirmations, quotes, and prayers of thanksgiv-ing to God as if our request has already been granted. When this test was presented to us long ago, we realized that God had a purpose in determining our degree of faith, trust, perseverance, humility, patience, and obedience. We decided that God wanted to see if we learned our lesson to trust the Creator uncondition-ally, no matter how dreadful things may have seemed.

We presented our financial package for the refinancing nine months before the note would come due. The banker had told us that the loan could not be extended under any circumstanc-es. We presented the financial documents I had prepared for different local banks, institutions, and brokers in other states. We were rejected by many financial brokers and bankers and received as many reasons why we could not accomplish the refinancing goals that we wanted and needed. Each time, we believed that God was working for our benefit and that everything—including all the rejections and delays—occurred for our good; we just had to wait for the right time and the right deal. We continued to pray and believe; one day, God sent us a messenger. We received a phone call from a friend who had worked with us for many years and provided us with numerous mortgages. He mentioned that by pure chance, he came across our name among his contacts list and felt compelled to call, even though so much time had elapsed since our last commu-nication. Strangely enough, he called just after we had received a rejection from the previous banker. I mentioned our intent to refinance the property during our conversation, and he offered to help.

9
FAITH IS THE BELIEF THAT GOD IS IN CONTROL – AND WHATEVER HAPPENS IS FOR THE BEST

The next day, we met and were convinced that God had sent the right person to assist us. After providing our friend with all the necessary documentation, he compiled a professional financial package, which he presented to every bank that poten-tially would be willing to work with us. Virtually every week, we received one rejection after another, until finally, after a few months, a local banker approached him and expressed an interest in refinancing that property. The banker and another two representatives came to our property, felt comfortable with the arrangement, and were willing to provide the required funding. After the banker went through the underwriting process, he requested that we meet with the bank's president to finalize the refinancing deal.

SUCCESS & PROSPERITY

They invited another banker who would provide us with the required additional funding to lower the mortgage rate with a long-term self-amortization. Everything was agreed upon when suddenly, the bank president asked to be excused. A few moments later, he returned and said, "I have to wait until tomorrow to make a decision." My wife and I looked at each other and said aloud, "I know that God is in control of our lives, and whatever will happen is going to be for the best."

The next day, the loan officer called our broker and said the deal was off. Despite the president's decision, our prayers never wavered, and we maintained our optimistic belief and faith in God, along with firm conviction. We believed that God was in control of all things and would provide the best guidance and direction.

The banker who would provide us with the participating mortgage called the broker to inquire whether he could move forward to get the approval with other banks. Five weeks later, he sent us documents to execute, stating that we had been approved for the participating portion. Then, he asked our broker whether he could send our approved package to a few banks interested in providing the other part of the loan. The broker agreed, and the banker eagerly shared the good news with us.

Two weeks later, the broker informed us that he found a bank with which we could transact business and asked whether we could meet the banker at the property. We accepted and were impressed by the bank representative's knowledge. The repre-sentative expressed approval of our facility and its operation. He then assured us of a "done deal" and said that the underwrit-ing and letter of commitment would be completed within a few days.

Two days passed, and the broker called again to tell me that another bank had expressed an interest in the loan. Therefore, he wanted to show our property to the second bank's represen-tative and the other banker, who already had the approval. We were amazed at how God worked in mysterious ways since we had been rejected so many times. Now, we had two banks from which to choose! The most important consideration was that God was in control, orchestrating our ultimate good.

A few weeks passed, and we continued to pray and believe that God would provide. To our surprise, we received letters of commitment from both banks simultaneously. We were in a quandary about which bank to choose, and we asked God for a sign. As we headed to one of the banks the following day, Esther was happy that God had provided us with the finances. At the same time, however, she was concerned that we would have to choose one bank over another, as we were very fond of both bankers, and their deal was almost identical. I reassured her that God was in control and had a purpose for us.

When we arrived at our destination, the bank's president cordially approached us and said, "Before you sign the papers and give us the check for the commitment, I have to ask you a question, and we can move forward according to your response." As we sat down, he continued. "I received a call from the other banker with whom you were simultaneously negotiating the deal. He just happens to be a friend of mine. It turns out that the other bank wants to participate fifty-fifty with us on the loan."

Esther couldn't believe her ears and repeatedly asked whether both banks would contribute to the venture. "Great! Hallelujah!" she declared when she knew that both banks would cooperate."This was an answer to my prayer!" she said.

We closed a couple of weeks later, and everything worked out for the best. The loan with these two banks and the other participating bank turned out to be a better deal with all that we required —and at a better rate and terms.

Many people ask us how we put faith into practice in our business dealings and transactions. Here is what I tell everyone who poses that question: According to our beliefs and the testimonies received from God in our life, we have concluded that God is the energy that created everything in this world and every soul incarnated on earth. Faith is like an electric plug. As long as the plug is connected to the outlet, the energy flows through and creates electricity, generating the necessary power for the electrical device to which it is connected to function. Therefore, we can use positive energy by being connected to God or remain unplugged and use our own power. When we are not plugged into the power that created us, we will eventually run out of energy. Either way, God loves us and watches us evolve in our own way.

God provides us with many signs to take our plug and connect it to the Creator's energy to enjoy the power and satisfaction of being part of the eternal or God energy. Once we do so, we will understand our purpose in life, and everything will begin to fall into place. Most likely, by being disconnected from God's outlet, we go through many trials and tribulations we sometimes create for ourselves by not having God present in the decision-making process. God allows things to happen to bring us to our senses, to return to our Creator, correct our mistakes, ask for forgiveness, and implement the plan that the Master of the Universe has prepared for us. With Divine intervention, we can succeed and have abundant health and happiness to become a channel for others in our Circle of Love. Therefore, do not wait any longer. Connect your plug to the boundless energy of God—the true outlet that will bring you victory in this world and peace in the world to come.

Lessons In Faith and God-given Destiny

As we demonstrated in this testimony (one of many yet to come), God allowed us to go through difficulties for a long time and closed many doors. Different bankers rejected us numerous times as a test of our faith to determine if we would maintain per-severance and keep the faith. We had to trust in God and know that our Creator was in control of our lives, always intending to provide the best outcome in our favor.

God orchestrated the best deal with everything that we needed and desired, but everything would not have come to pass if we had become depressed and doubtful or if we had questioned God's purpose. We never asked, "Why are we having difficul-ties closing our deal? Why have we experienced so many rejec-tions, and why is it taking so long?" These negative thoughts and questions would have taken us away from our God-given destiny that would have obstructed the Divine plan for us.

Maintaining a positive, faithful outlook is not always easy when everything is going against us. However, that is what every one of us needs to do daily as we confront various obstacles, even though we may be going through financial or health dif-ficulties, challenging family matters, career or job decisions, etc. In this way, with faith in God as our provider, we will reap the fruits of prosperity and success. It is always essential that when we talk to our friends and family, we always express our gratitude for what God has done in our lives. In so doing, we give great satisfaction to God. We are not taking the glory unto ourselves but, instead, giving the glory to the Creator, and that testimony may inspire others also to place their trust in God.

Although we had no idea how we would resolve our difficul-ties, God knew—and that is what faith is all about.

Faith in God works in all aspects of our lives—in ways big and small, in professional or personal dealings with doctors, lawyers, judges, realtors, college admissions staff, at the office, and a host of other interpersonal exchanges. We have been very fortunate because, throughout all our ups and downs, our faith continues to grow, and we thank God for presenting us with daily tests that we have been able to transform into testimonies and victories.

We have been tested in innumerable ways, and we have many personal stories that we wish to share about how our trials and tribulations have served to bring us closer to God. Amen.

We exist as **One World Family**, all creations of God, and we must treat each other with respect and love, regardless of race, national origin, or religion.

CHAPTER 2

A TESTIMONY OF OBEDIENCE THAT TURNED INTO A FOREVER LOVE

It is no exaggeration to state that the greatest manifestation of God at work in our lives is the love we have shared during our fifty-three years of marriage and counting—forever. When I was just turning seventeen, Aunt Raquel and Uncle Angel gave me a birthday present: money in an envelope. The envelope also included a very interesting message that read as follows:

> *Marcos, you are of an age now which calls for caring for your broken front teeth. Not only should you fix them for health reasons, but also to look presentable to girls your age. Upon reading this note, I approached my aunt and said, "Tía, I give all the money I earn to my father to administer and tend to our ex penses.*

"I understand, and you are doing the correct thing, Marcos, but you should still speak to your father about fixing your front teeth." I followed through and spoke to my father, who agreed to give me an allowance every week from my paycheck to save for the care of my teeth. When I accumulated enough money, I visited the local dentist around the corner. Luckily, the doctor accepted installment payments, which made it easier to undertake the expense. Upon completing the dental work, I looked like a different person—my natural self again, and I felt more confident.

With spring approaching, Aunt Raquel prophesized that soon I would meet a very beautiful girl who would be my soul mate. "She will be a brunette, sweet and shy," she told me.

A week passed, and on a Saturday morning, my brother Leon and I were on our way to the laundromat on the corner. Suddenly, we spotted Sarita, a neighbor walking with her niece, a stunning brunette.

As Sarita and her niece approached, Leon exclaimed, "That girl coming toward us is my girl."

"No way!" I protested. "She has all of the characteristics that Tía Raquel mentioned. She said that I would soon meet my soul mate."

"You know that according to our custom, the older sibling marries first, and the younger one has to wait," Leon insisted.

"No way," I insisted. "Since Tía Raquel told me I would meet my soul mate, I will obey and follow through. Please do not interfere. Besides, at twenty-one, you are too old for her. She looks about fourteen or fifteen, and I am seventeen, just the right age."

While we were immersed in this conversation, Sarita and her niece came closer; Sarita said "hello," and introduced Esther as her niece.

"Esther lives in the Bronx and has come with her sister to spend the weekend with us," she explained. Instantly, I continued the conversation.

"Hello, my name is Marcos, and this is my older brother, Leon," I said. I would like to invite you to join us at the temple tonight. The Maccabi (a young Sephardic Jewish organization) has organized a get-together at 7 p.m. so that all the young Jewish neighborhood residents can get to know one another. There will be refreshments, dancing, and other activities. I would love you to join us to get to know one another. It's going to be fun." I did not mince words.

10
WHEN DESTINY IS BEFORE YOU, SAY WHAT YOU NEED TO SAY. DO NOT HOLD BACK

"Esther, I think you should go," Sarita chimed in, noting that her niece did not say a word.

Esther shook her head, indicating that she wanted to leave. *She is so beautiful, but she seems very shy, just like Tia Raquel had prognosticated a couple of weeks earlier*, I thought.

Later that evening, my brother and I attended the event with our sister, Fortuna, and older brother, Pepe, at the synagogue. We looked around for Esther, but there was no sign of her. Suddenly, I spotted her entering with Sarita. My heart raced, and I could scarcely contain myself. Struggling to gain composure, I approached Sarita and her niece and addressed Esther; I said, "I'm so glad you could make it! You look so beautiful!" Esther smiled and looked at her aunt.

I had better ask her to dance before Leon beats me to it, I said to myself. Mustering all my courage, I said, "Will you give me the honor of dancing with me? You look so pretty in that dress, and we must show it off."

Esther smiled and nodded shyly. As we began to dance, I was struck by the fact that the beautiful girl had a speaking voice and could sing, too. She knew every song by heart. As we danced, I listened to Esther's lovely distinctive tones, and even though she didn't speak to me, I felt that somehow, I had known this girl for a very long time. There was a definite connection between us. *Tía Raquel's prophesy is becoming a reality*, I said to myself.

11
SPOKEN WORDS OF WISDOM ARE THE ECHOES OF GOD'S VOICE

Before the event ended, Sarita came to retrieve Esther. As they had agreed, Sarita arrived early to check in on her niece. When she saw that Esther was having a pleasant time, she said, "Take your time. I will wait until the gathering disperses."

Esther danced one more dance with me before she had to leave. "When will we see each other again?" I asked.

"I am returning to the Bronx tomorrow morning," Esther replied.

"But don't worry because she'll return next weekend," Sarita said reassuringly.

Grabbing a pen and paper, I wrote down my telephone number, saying, "Please let me know when you return."

The day after the event, I visited Aunt Raquel and Uncle Angel. I was so excited to tell them that Tía's prediction had actually happened. "I am also very grateful that you convinced me to fix my teeth and that the dentist could implant temporary caps before the event—and at just the right time – on the Friday before I met the girl that captured my heart. The improvement in my appearance gave me renewed confidence, though, in truth, I never felt terrible about my broken teeth.

As all these exciting events took place, I observed God's hand in helping me grow in faith and obedience and paying attention to Aunt Raquel's teaching and guidance.

12
GOD'S HAND IS IN THE DETAILS. SOMETIMES, IT MANIFESTS THROUGH THE TEACHING AND GUIDANCE OF OTHERS

The week went by very slowly for me. By all appearances, I had already committed my heart to the girl I knew was my soul mate. Every night, I would think to myself, I wonder what she is doing now. Is she thinking of me? I would lift my thoughts to God in gratitude for giving me my soul mate. I would say, "God, we are so young, and I don't know what love should feel like, but if this is love, it feels wonderful, and I am constantly thinking about her, wanting to be with her all the time. I wonder if she feels the same way."

Each day, I went to work during the day and high school night classes three times a week. On my days off from school, I visited my aunt, eager to learn more about faith, love, per-sistence, and the world to come. Of course, I also wanted to discover more about Esther.

SUCCESS & PROSPERITY

Because of Aunt Raquel's intuitive sixth sense, she was able to provide some insight. "Esther is timid but also very intelligent, and she loves her family very much. Those are excellent qualities for a girl to have."

Saturday finally arrived, and I awoke, dressed elegantly, and went to the laundromat intending to run into Esther; but to my disappointment, I didn't see her. However, I remembered Aunt Raquel's instructions: "Be persistent, have faith, and God will reward you," she said.

After taking the laundry home, I went out again to see if I could spot her on the street. "Do you know where Sarita lives?" I asked the neighbor walking on the same street where I had met her and her niece. Then, I saw another neighbor whose name was Jack. He approached, and I asked him the same question.

13
PERSISTENCE, WHEN COUPLED WITH FAITH, IS THE MOST IMPORTANT FACTOR WHEN YOU ARE SEARCHING FOR A SOUL MATE

"She is my sister," Jack replied.
"Did Esther return this weekend?" I wanted to know.
"Yes, I believe that she did," Jack answered.
"Can you tell me where Sarita lives?" I persisted.
"Come, I will take you there," Jack offered, leading the way.

14
GOD ORCHESTRATES THE UNION OF SOULS.
IT IS UP TO US TO FOLLOW THROUGH

Soon, Jack arrived at Sarita's home, and I followed close to his side. Sarita welcomed us warmly, and to my delight, as I stepped into the house, I saw the girl of my dreams. I had a strange feeling in the pit of my stomach as I stared at Esther while she glanced back with an air of contentment. Sarita invited me in as Jack left to run some errands. Esther's Uncle Enrique was also there and greeted me cordially.

"I have to go, too," I said, trying to curtail my enthusiasm. "But I'd like to come back later and take Esther bowling if she wants to go."

Sarita turned to her niece for an answer, and Esther nodded.

Elated, I said, "I will return at 7:00 p.m., after dinner."

Keeping my promise, I promptly arrived at Sarita's home at 7:00 p.m., reassuring her that Esther and I would return, according to her instruction, by 9:00 p.m. As we soon discov-ered, the bowling alley was closed for repairs. So, we just rode about, talking and enjoying each other's company.

"You are so beautiful, Esther. I enjoyed our dance last week and love being with you. I think about you all the time, espe-cially before going to sleep at night. I pray to God to guide me to show you that you're my soul mate, and God has enabled us to meet again in this world together, have a family, and live a life of love, abundance, health, and prosperity.

Esther uttered not one word but just kept inhaling and exhaling.

"Since you're not saying anything, I will ask God to send me a spirit to help me understand the language of inhaling and exhaling."

Esther laughed but did not give any indication of her thoughts or feelings. Finally, when we arrived at Sarita's apartment at 9:00, we stood on the stairs outside. "I enjoyed every moment of our time together. Do you think we can see each other tomorrow?"

Without answering, Esther just shrugged her shoulders.

"Good night, Esther," I said, moving closer, trying to kiss her, but she backed away.

"Okay. Maybe, it is too soon," I said respectfully. Turning and walking down the stairs, I looked back to see whether Esther had gone inside and was happy to notice her standing on the top step. I told myself, If she turns to look back at me, that means she likes me.

She did, and I smiled to myself. I'll just keep putting into practice everything Aunt Raquel taught me and believe that all of this is part of God's plan. I just have to keep believing.

On Sunday morning, there I was, ringing the doorbell to Sarita's house, asking for Esther. Uncle Enrique came out and politely told me that Esther had gone to Jack's house and returned to the Bronx.

15
BE PATIENT. GOD HAS A PLAN. YOU JUST HAVE TO KEEP BELIEVING

"Thank you, Enrique. You are a very nice man," I noted, taking my leave.

When I arrived home, I confided in my mother, Lina, about my feelings for Esther and that Aunt Raquel predicted that she was my soul mate.

"Take your time, my son. You are still very young. I pray that God will guide you in everything you do," my mother said soothingly, maintaining a realistic view of the circumstances.

Heeding her advice, I went on with my schooling and work, constantly thinking about Esther. I couldn't wait for another week to go by before I saw her again. In my heart, she was the one. At last, when Saturday rolled around, I jumped at the chance to see Esther and take her to the park. It was late afternoon, and the sky was overcast, but the only sensation that I could feel was the warmth of my heart, radiating outward toward Esther and my fervent wish to win her affection. While we were at the park, we sat down on a bench, and I continued to shower Esther with compliments. These expressions were met with a persistent silent treatment and intermittent inhaling and exhaling. Soon, I came to interpret this reaction as feelings of love. I even showed her the poems

I composed in her honor, and as far as I could tell, she loved them; but her only response was the slow, measured cadence of her breathing.

"I pray that God will give me the ability to understand the language of inhaling and exhaling," I said, at which point Esther blithely laughed out loud.

"I love the way you laugh!" I exclaimed.

It started to rain at that moment—a slight drizzle slowly falling to the pavement. Esther got up and began to walk out of the park to avoid getting wet, and I followed.

16
WHEN IT RAINS, SOMETIMES GOD IS POURING DOWN LOVE. WATCH FOR GOD'S SIGNS

Just as we were leaving the park, a torrential downpour descended on us, the likes of which we had never seen or ex-perienced before. I held Esther, protecting her from slipping into the enormous puddles that rapidly filled our path. As we hurried along, the water began to accumulate in the street, and by the time we reached Sarita's house, the water was up to our knees. Sarita hurried us inside, saying that she had been worried about us. We were drenched, and Esther immediately ran into the bathroom to change while Sarita gave me a pair of Uncle Enrique's pajamas to wear while my clothes dried. Sarita gave her niece and me some hot milk and aspirin to prevent us from catching a cold and blankets to warm us up. Esther and I sat in the living room and watched television in this state of comfort and security.

A little past 10:00 p.m., after the rain had stopped, we heard a knock at the door. My mother entered in a state of height-ened concern. "Marcos, I was so worried about you," she said, looking at me with a solemn expression.

"He came here because he and my niece got soaked in the rain. He was just waiting for his clothes to dry," Sarita explained.

"Marcos, you could have called me to tell me where you were. Please do not leave me in suspense again.

17
DO NOT LET LOVE BE AN EXCUSE TO RELIEVE YOU FROM YOUR OBLIGATIONS

"Okay, Mamita. I will never do that again and make you worry," I said, rising to hug her.

Before I left to go home, I gave Esther my telephone number and asked her to call me during the week after 8:30 p.m. When Esther returned to the Bronx, she followed through on that request. I was so delighted because I had a chance to hear her speak on the phone far more than she did in person. Occasionally, she would intersperse the conversation with her usual inhaling and exhaling, at the sound of which I would remark, "I love it. This is fantastic. Even on the phone, you're able to share your expressions of love through inhaling and exhaling."

In my heart, I felt what Esther could not admit – even to herself: our feeling of love was mutual. If that had not been the case, she would never have sacrificed to go to the pay phone at the corner drugstore to call me. When time ran out, I would call her back. My father, Israel, would complain that his son was spending too much time on the phone; but I just couldn't help myself. Sometimes, after Esther visits Brooklyn, I would ask her to call me upon her return to the Bronx. We would remain on the phone for a long time. Noting this, my father would comment, "Here they spend the weekends together and then speak on the phone for a long while when Esther returns to the Bronx."

Without question, love was in the air. As time passed, Esther could not visit her aunt in Brooklyn every weekend, so I asked if I could come to the Bronx and see her since it was very difficult to go a long time without being in her company. Esther agreed, and we were able to forge an even closer bond. I met Esther's parents, Leon and Lea, and her sister, Raquel. Everyone was so kind and hospitable, and Lea's cooking was so delicious that I would eat every morsel, to her delight.

Esther and I would go to the park only a couple of blocks from her house, and Rachel would always come along. Over time, I got to know Rachel and grew to love her immensely. I thought she was funny, enthusiastic, and extremely smart for her age. Our times together were always memorable, and I always looked forward to our next meeting. My over one-hour subway ride from Brooklyn to the Bronx was no trouble when I thought of the benefits of seeing my two favorite girls, and with every meeting, I grew more and more attached and devoted to Esther.

Soon, we began to date as boyfriend and girlfriend officially. Aunt Raquel and Uncle Angel took us in their car to many places in Brooklyn, Manhattan, and Long Island. Before my birthday in December, I approached Aunt Raquel and asked, "Tía, what would you say about me marrying Esther?"

"We will support you in everything that you want to do. The two of you should talk it over, pray about it, and if you mutually decide to marry, you must talk to your parents and get their approval," Aunt Raquel advised.

18
LOVE INVOLVES SACRIFICES, BUT THE GIVE-AND-TAKE IS PART OF GOD'S TEST OF TRUE LOVE

As it turned out, my parents had some reservations about the marriage due to their custom of marrying off the older son first. At twenty-five, Pepe, my older brother, did not have a girlfriend because he was timid around women.

"Papá," I began with love and respect in my voice. "I un-derstand that there are traditions in every culture and religion. However, Esther and I have been going steady for almost a year, and although we are young, we are mature and love each other. We are ready to take on responsibilities, have a family, and face life together.

"But how will both of you pay for the wedding?" my father answered.

SUCCESS & PROSPERITY

"When we believe, God always provides. Also, Tía Raquel predicted that Esther would be my soul mate, and we shouldn't let that opportunity pass by; but we need your blessing first, and the rest will follow."

"I give you my blessing," my father replied upon hearing my earnest plea. "Come with Esther and work in my factory and I'll put you on the payroll," he suggested.

19
WHEN WE BELIEVE, GOD ALWAYS PROVIDES

Esther and I agreed and went to work in the factory, learned how to sew and press, and were very productive when working with every kind of specialty machine.

My father encouraged us to open a joint savings account to help pay for the wedding and told me that he did not want me to contribute any more money to the expenses for our house. He wanted us to save for our wedding. Aunt Raquel and Uncle Angel promised to assist however they could, and Esther's and my parents graciously chipped in. Her Aunt Sarita and Uncle Enrique offered to supply the furniture for our apartment (given that Uncle Enrique was in the furniture business).

We requested that the engagement take place on my birthday, and everyone involved readily assented. The whole family and the rabbi's neighbor who lived in the apartment below were in attendance. We were overwhelmed by the testimonies of belief and faith that God illuminates the way and always puts the right people in the path of those who seek divine guidance.

When family and community members got wind of our engagement news, everyone was surprised that we would wed at such a young age. Others were skeptical that the marriage would last, and others said we would not be able to make ends meet, but Esther and I ignored such comments. We were determined to believe that God would see us through and focused on the promise the Creator gave us through Aunt Raquel. The song "Too Young" by Nat King Cole played the soundtrack of our lives and became our favorite song.

On our wedding day, August 15, the most beautiful, simple ceremony took place, with many family and friends in atten-dance. God paved the way for my cousin Albert (who was in culinary school at the time) to come in from Dallas with Pepe, our other cousin, and they assisted with the meal preparations. What a great blessing! Everyone had a wonderful time, with plenty of food and beverages to go around—not to mention rejoicing and celebrating our union.

20
GOD ALWAYS PUTS THE RIGHT PEOPLE IN THE PATH OF THOSE WHO SEEK DIVINE GUIDANCE

After we bid farewell to our family and guests, we hopped into the 1956 black Ford God had provided us before the wedding. We headed to a hotel in Manhattan for one night before leaving on our honeymoon to Atlantic City, New Jersey, the next day. On our way from Brooklyn to New York, someone who appeared to be drunk behind the wheel almost crashed into us; but miraculously, it was a near miss. Pulling to the side of the road, we prayed and thanked God for protecting us and called forth continued divine intervention in our new Circle of Love.

Our first evening as a married couple was marred by the breaking of a bathroom pipe that soaked the hotel room floor, causing water to deluge the entire room. Floods seemed to beset our courtship and the first night of marriage. Perhaps, those events signaled the showering of God's love and abundance in our lives. Through it all, we kept calm, called the front desk, and requested that a maintenance expert come to fix the pipe. They came right away, and within two hours, it was repaired, and the water was removed. We laughed about these experiences, but at the same time, we thanked God as we began our honeymoon.

**21
NEVER HEED THE VOICES
OF DOUBT AND NEGATIVITY.
INSTEAD, PLACE YOUR FAITH
IN GOD AND BE
ASSURED THAT GOD
IS WORKING FOR YOUR BENEFIT**

"Well, we certainly will never forget our honeymoon," I told my beautiful wife.

Esther laughed and breathed a sigh of relief.

"This is a test, and God is going to see us victorious," I added.

The next day, we left for Atlantic City. Fortunately, the weather held out. The sun was shining on our first day as husband and wife. The Trymore Hotel on the boardwalk in Atlantic City was lovely, and the fresh, salty air filled our lungs and senses. The staff assigned us to room 815. We took that as a divine sign that God wanted us to remember our wedding date, 8/15. The room was spacious and comfortable, and we savored every moment, creating great memories that we still remember.

Upon arriving home to our simple Brooklyn apartment, we resolved to keep our wonderful honeymoon memories alive for the rest of our lives. We also promised never to go to sleep angry at one another. If we had different opinions about something or someone, we would communicate freely and try to resolve issues before we closed our eyes since we realize that tomorrow is not promised to anyone. We also pledged to kiss one another's wedding rings as a gesture of love and commitment to perpetu-ate our Circle of Love forever. Finally, we mutually promised to trust in God, regardless of the tests we would confront—whether these involved financial, health, business, or personal matters- and infuse faith and trust in divine guidance for every major decision. That pledge has continued for a lifetime.

Trusting In God to Find Our Soul Mate

When we are young, it isn't easy to practice patience. We all have ideas, dreams, and goals that we wish to fulfill, and in most cases, we want them to happen NOW. In our haste, we often forget that God has a plan that may be different than ours, with completely different timing. In these instances, it is important not to act impulsively but instead listen to the little voice inside us – the whispers of God, telling us how and when to act.

My Aunt Raquel had a special gift of clairvoyance. She always trusted in God and taught me the importance of faith. She taught me the art of patience and faithful adherence to God's will and wishes. As the Master of our mission on earth, God is the ultimate orchestrator of our destinies and how our lives play out on the journey. I was so fortunate to have my aunt as my teacher and mentor to guide and help me find my true, forever love.

Sometimes, young people act irrationally, but in my case, I had a patient, loving teacher who taught me to wait on God's time. The Great Architect constructs our future according to wisdom far surpassing our own. So, while waiting to find love, it is best to employ measured patience and revert to faith (rather than act in haste) to reap the best long -term benefits. None of these rewards is more meaningful than finding "the One" with whom we spend our most significant, cherished moments in this life, and for eternity, we will rejoice in the peace granted to us by God when we have fulfilled our missions on earth.

Not every soul has the blessing and privilege of finding a soul mate. Those who fall in love and decide to wed have been placed in each other's paths by God for a purpose. Perhaps, our companions/partners might serve as tests of our patience, tem-perament, faith, self-control, and other characteristics. If we accept that everything we experience is a test, we can engage in soul- searching to identify our mistakes, rectify them, or assess what we may have done wrong before or in a previous life. By accepting God's tests, we acquire all the necessary tools to succeed and attain happiness.

By directing our lives toward God and requesting God's as-sistance, we will begin to receive victories, to see each day dif-ferently, and therefore, our lives will start to turn around for the better. God will grant us wisdom and peace and give us the spirit of discernment and all the spiritual armor we need to turn our tests into testimonies. If it is God's will that we find our soul mate, either now or later, we must always do our best in every circumstance and continue to strive toward our goals. If, on the other hand, we attempt to accomplish everything on our own without inviting God into our lives for all of our decision-mak-ing, we then guide ourselves by our own limited knowledge, which may cause us to experience negativity and prolong our tests. The choices belong to us.

Be in tune with God

... AND THE WAY WILL BE MADE CLEAR

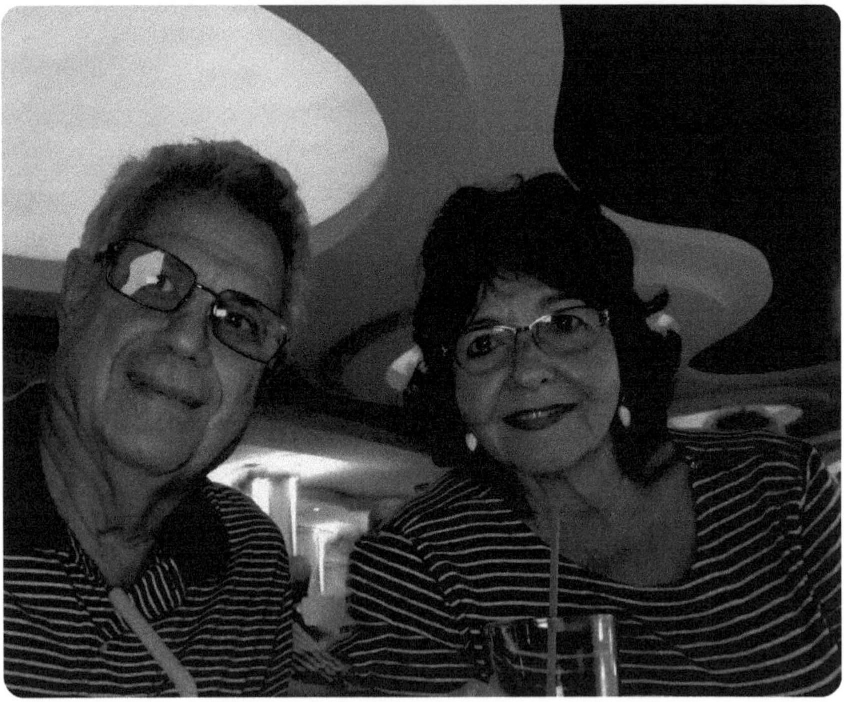

In These Moments

I need not say a word. You are here, and so am I. Therefore,
in these moments, we can just BE—TOGETHER.
My happiness is complete, now and forever.

We need not prove anything. We are enough.

I need not try. The present with you takes care
of everything—God ensures that.

Eternity speaks in a whisper. We have always listened.
Finding each other was proof. I am grateful.

Mordechai and Esther Fintz

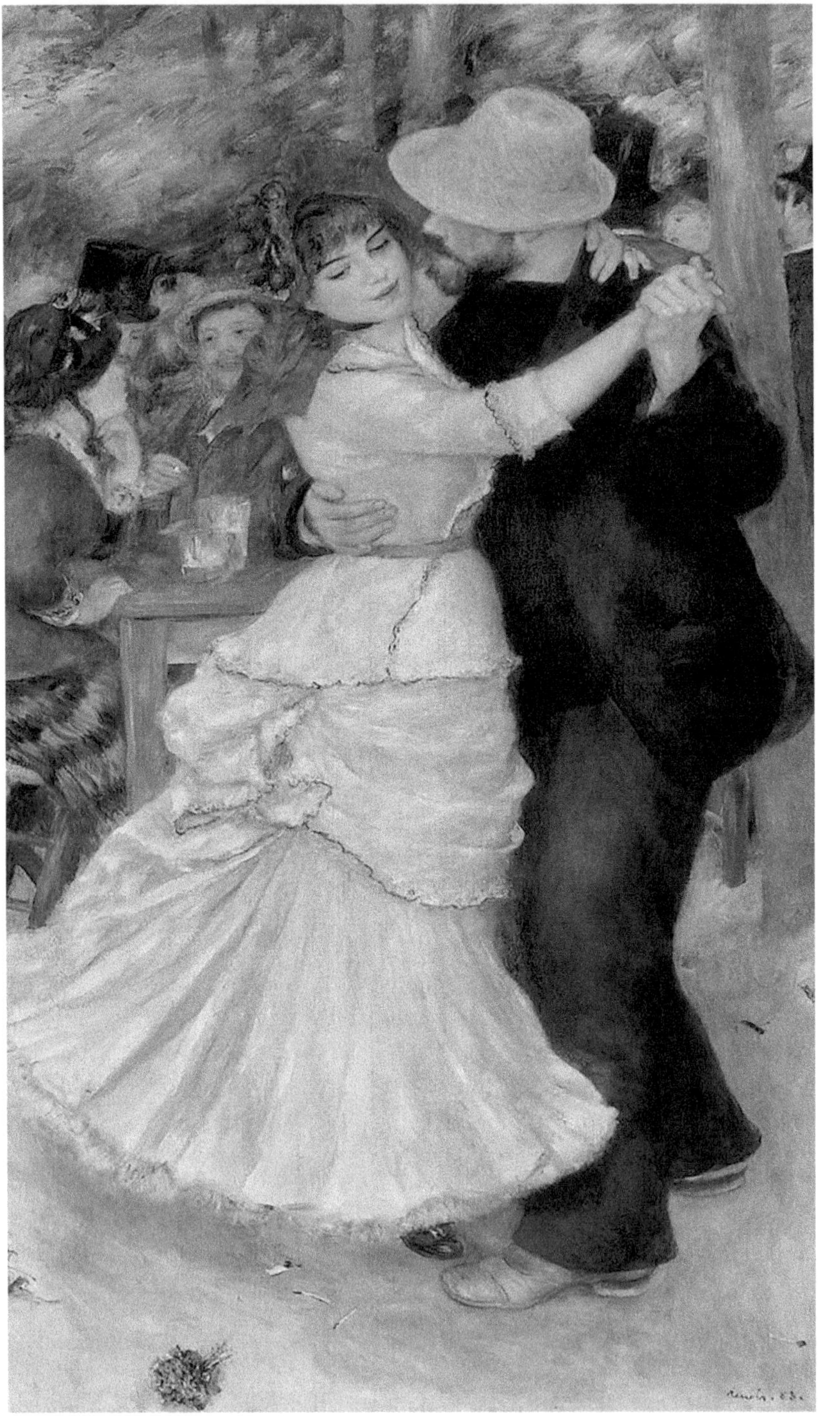

CHAPTER 3

WHAT MAKES A MARRIAGE SUCCESSFUL?

The Benefits of Finding Our Soul mate

When we enter the world, our spirits are incarnated into a new baby, born into a family that becomes our Circle of Love. God has predestined that in this Circle of Love, our family members will help us grow, and we will have absorbed our family's ways, beliefs, and manners. When we grow into young adults capable of making our own decisions, we start questioning all of the influences from our parents and family, experience certain desires, and seek answers to our questions that we sometimes cannot find within our families. We also entertain questions that sometimes differ from our parents' example. According to God's plan, we learn to grow into what we are destined to become. Our Circle of Love will support or promote our spiritual development or sometimes influence and force us to believe and follow their ways of life. At the same time, we may be born into challenging circumstances and dys-functional families with many burdens. God orchestrates such challenges to lead us to fulfill our purposes, which are huge tests we must overcome and turn into victories.

22
CREATING OUR OWN CIRCLE OF LOVE IS PART OF OUR SPIRITUAL GROWTH

Each person has a mission, and if we come to know God at an early age, the Divine will guide us during those difficult circum-stances and help us grow spiritually. Each of us has a unique character and a different mission, and we are created by God through our parents. Throughout our lifetimes, we must develop and grow with the understanding that God has a purpose for everything—including placing us in our own Circle of Love. With time, we come to understand that everything works out for the best.

When we reach young adulthood, our materialistic instincts compel us to seek sexual satisfaction, which we confuse with the true purpose of the companionship of the person with whom we will spend the rest of our lives. Once we connect with that individual, we can create our own Circle of Love. In young adulthood, most people are also influenced by friends, family, and all types of media that wrongly identify life's true meaning and purpose. We need to sift through these influences to determine which ones are good for us and which are not. We must learn how to pray, meditate and be patient by resting in God's guidance so that our decisions do not hinder our spiritual growth. To reap the fruits of love, we must continue on the right path to finding our soul mate, creating our own circle of love, and attaining peace, abundance, and happiness.

23
OUR SEARCH FOR OUR SOUL MATE STARTS AS EARLY AS OUR YOUNG ADULTHOOD

My wife and I have gone through many of those processes. Fifty-nine years have passed since we married and formed our Circle of Love. One of our most essential ingredients for success in our marriage is our God- given opportunity to have found each other as soul mates at an early age and to have had—and always continue to enjoy—the opportunity to share the love, challenges, tests, and blessings that God has poured into us. We have also grown by helping one another through life's various phases. In the process of growing in the art of loving one another, developing an attitude of compromise, tolerance, and balance is imperative. We must accept each other as indi-vidual souls, brought together by the power of love that unites us. We can then form our own Circle of Love and help each other grow while rejoicing in God's blessings.

"Soul mate" is an uncommon term that not many understand or use in daily conversations. The reason is that we are trained to only focus on physical attraction or material benefit and security based on wealth, looks, position, or influence, and we fail to concern ourselves with the most important issue: searching for the individual who will be our soul mate and help us in this world to be a better person, create our Circle of Love, have a family, prosper, attain abundance and the ultimate reward— the attainment of eternal peace in the world to come – together.

> **24**
> **SOUL MATES SHOULD NOT BE CHOSEN BASED ON PHYSICAL ATRACTION ALONE, BUT INSTEAD, ON THE SPIRITUAL VALUES AND BELIEFS THAT WILL HELP THE COUPLE TO BE BETTER PEOPLE AND ATTAIN HAPPINESS IN THIS WORLD AND IN THE WORLD TO COME**

People often confront us and ask: "What does it mean to meet our soul mate, and how do we know when that happens?" Our answers are simple. Below, we present a few suggestions for the reader to consider when searching for a soul mate. Read, analyze, and meditate on each one, thinking about each point to determine whether any one or all of them can be helpful in your life. If not, ask yourself, "What can I take from this that will benefit me in the future when I get married?"

Pray and Trust in God

When we pray, we open our channels, and God shows us the way to be at the correct place or meet the right person who could be our soul mate. When we are young and do not have experi-ence in making good decisions, we tend to rush without evalu-ating the options that God places before us. This can happen when, for example, we fall in love based on physical attraction, material possessions, personal wealth, or professional status without considering the influence and guidance of our souls. We can ask for the opinions of our family and friends, but we cannot allow anyone to influence us with negative thoughts, put pressure on us, or put us down. We must always rest on God's direct guidance through the small voice inside us and rely on the fact that God created us to be unique.

> **25**
> **WHEN CHOOSING A SOUL MATE, RELY ON YOUR INTUITION; IGNORE EXTERNAL NEGATIVITY AND DOUBT**

We must recognize that we are valuable and have everything it takes to live a life of happiness. We can also ask God to provide us with signs that serve as tests to ensure we are heading in the right direction. We must understand that we cannot change the people we meet—even those we love. Only God can help each one to change.

Sometimes, we commit for the wrong reasons. For example, family members may pressure their loved ones to marry to start a family and provide grandchildren, or some may feel compelled to marry for financial security or because of their age.

The only valid and proper reason to get married is out of love and respect for one another, regardless of education, back-ground, religion, or financial status. Each person must feel the love and attraction that creates mutual respect and willingness to help one another. Those are the qualities of true soul mates. We must trust in God and each other, knowing that God is always working for our good in times of trial and tribulation. In every relationship, both partners come from different Circles of Love, with distinct opinions and mindsets, but when challenges arise, that is when we are tested, and we need to commit ourselves to our long- term relationship to overcome any and all tests that God puts before us. We must openly and sincerely communi-cate with one another and share ideas with love and respect. Sometimes when one of the spouses is more committed to main-taining trust in God than the other, the couple must exercise tolerance and help each other in these circumstances. God has given us a spirit of faith, not fear, doubt, and stress. Whenever we allow the spirit of darkness, anxiety, and doubt to enter our minds, we begin to complain about everything and experience uncertainty regarding one another's actions. The relationship inevitably suffers when this occurs, and our love is tested. We must revoke all those thoughts and feelings and return to God, the provider of goodness, love, and kindness that enables us to praise and validate one another.

When we cooperate and commit to a co-equal partnership with our spouse, we can embark on a journey of love and har-monious living—together. Nothing is stronger than a bond of love created by mutual respect, honesty, understanding, love, and compassion.

26
**IN TIMES OF CRISIS —
AS AT ALL TIMES —
SHARE IDEAS WITH
YOUR SOUL MATE WITH
LOVE AND RESPECT,
AND ALLOW GOD
TO ACT AS YOUR COMPASS**

We must have faith in God and be patient, always paying attention to the other person's needs and determining whether the individual we choose as our life partner will be there for us as we are for them. To succeed, relationships cannot be one-sided but must be co-equal so that each person acts independently and, at the same time, works together with their soul mate. In this way, the blessings of God will be present, and the couple can help each other fulfill their missions. Mutual acknowledgment of needs, hopes, and dreams is a crucial element in a success-ful marriage, and whatever challenges confront either or both, the couple must stand together as a pillar of strength against adversity, always trusting in God and the fact that Divine inter-vention will turn trials into lessons and lessons into victories. It is essential to practice humility with our fellow human beings. Such a practice begins with our soul mate. Once we identify the soul with whom we want to spend our earthly life and into eternity, we must discover our mate's likes and dislikes by being open with one another. Honest communication paves the way for a healthier relationship and mutual inner peace. Although we are one with our soul mate, we have different souls, and we come from a separate Circle of Love with our own customs, practices, and habits. Our spirits also come with different missions God programmed into us to help one another. Therefore, to grow spiritually and live a happy life, we must discover these various practices and habits before declaring someone our soul mate.

> **27**
> **TO SUCCEED IN OUR RELATIONSHIPS, WE CANNOT BE CLOSE-MINDED BUT, RATHER, WE MUST WORK TOGETHER AND HELP EACH OTHER. WE WILL THEN FEEL THE PRESENCE OF GOD'S BLESSINGS**

Once we find the person to whom we are attracted, fall in love with their physical appearance, values, and beliefs, and feel comfortable with that person as our soul mate, then before we make future plans, we should discuss personal habits to avoid friction and arguments at a later date. The following are some examples.

Our Sleeping Habits

Sometimes, when two people meet and fall in love, they fail to discuss which side of the bed each one would prefer when they marry. At times, their preference may be the same side, in which case they may not be willing to compromise or accommodate one another. I recall that Esther and I discussed this issue before our marriage, and I was happy to discover that we did not have any conflict of preferences. That was a great blessing. However, as calm as my wife is in her sleep, I am as restless (a circumstance out of my control). In that respect, Esther had to learn to adapt to the situation.

> **28**
> **OPEN COMMUNICATION, HONESTY, AND WILLINGNESS TO CULTIVATE MUTUALLY SHARED VALUES AND DREAMS ARE THE HALLMARKS OF A GREAT AND LASTING PARTNERSHIP**

Our Food Preferences

Here is another important subject that creates more argumentation than many other subjects among couples—particularly newlyweds.

I recall that Esther and I used to go to various restaurants when we were dating. I would typically order steak. I also used to add a lot of salt, whereas my wife preferred not to do so. Before I even tasted my steak, I would add salt, while Esther looked at me with a surprised expression and remarked, "Too much salt is not good for your body." I had a similar taste for sugar in my coffee (five packs), but Esther never took any sugar at all. We discussed these issues, and I realized that I would be the one to compromise when we got married because my wife was not about to cook with sugar and salt. So, I stopped putting salt on my steak before tasting it and cut down on my sugar to two packs. Luckily for me, sugar substitutes came on the market years later, and two packs were equivalent to five.

**29
TO AVOID UNNECESSARY
CONFLICTS, DISCUSS
YOUR BELIEFS AND
PREFERENCES OPENLY
WITH YOUR SOUL MATE
TO FORMULATE YOUR
OWN RULES WITHIN THE MARRIAGE**

Our Place of Worship, Family Meetings, and Our Children's Religious Upbringing

This is the most challenging and delicate matter that soul mates must overcome. Even if they have similar belief systems, they may attend various places of worship while growing up, and that subject must be addressed before marriage. In other cases, the couple may have been born in different Circles of Love, uniquely worshipping and believing in God. This is another of God's tests determin-ing whether the couple can unify their Circle of Love without misunderstandings or conflicts of opinion.

The families of two people in love must meet each other, es-pecially the respective parents. If the couple does not share the news of their love and intentions with their parents, the latter may find fault with the chosen partner and discourage their union. Surface appearances might obscure the new prospec-tive family member's true essence—who they are inside. This topic reminds me of the movie *Beauty and the Beast,* which we have seen many times and evokes beautiful memories of our granddaughter's fourth birthday. On that special occasion, our daughter-in-law orchestrated a Beauty and the Beast theme party for her, and we helped her to hire actors to perform in character and sing songs from the film in front of all the guests. The celebration was outstanding, and we still talk about it to this day. A few months ago (twenty-five years later), we watched the movie again, and the message remained the same: although we may look different on the outside and come from distinct backgrounds and social levels, we all have beautiful souls on the inside.

30
TO AVOID PERSONAL CONFLICTS, RELIGIOUS EDUCATION AND PRACTICES SHOULD BE AGREED UPON BEFORE THE CHILDREN ARE BORN

> **31**
> **RIDE OUT THE STORM TOGETHER AS A COUPLE AND DON'T ALLOCATE BLAME TO OTHERS FOR ANY DIFFICULTIES THAT MAY ARISE. SEE EACH OTHER THROUGH TO VICTORY**

Religious Education and Practices

Once a couple marries and has children, what religious instruction will they receive, and what faith will they practice as they grow and mature? I know some very loving couples who have difficulties resolving this issue, and in the absence of a solution, they don't attempt to choose their place of worship or an agreed- upon means of faithful practice for their children. In opting not to choose, they avoid the pressures of doing so. The children sometimes become agnostic or without a structured belief system in these cases. Therefore, the parents should decide at the outset how they wish to raise their family. This does not mean, however, that each parent should enforce their own religious practices to negate or contradict the other. Before confronting such an important decision, the couple should pray and ask God for guidance, or if they are already in that situation, they can begin at any time to make a concerted effort toward a solution. Each one must be willing to adapt to their mutual decision, and they should not discuss the matter in front of their parents and siblings. Doing so will only complicate the issue.

Place of Residence

The simple decision about where to live as a couple can become complicated if partners do not employ patience, understanding, and compromise. One set of parents might pressure the couple to move as close to them as possible so that when the children come, they can help out. Other parents want to provide financial support and shelter until the couple can get on their feet.

Suppose the couple has to sacrifice and accept their parents' offer of room and board temporarily. In that case, they should not hesitate and do their best to maintain peace and harmony with their parents while waiting to move into their own dwelling.

Follow the Principle of One Family

To create a success-ful marriage, the two united souls must commit to each other. They must promise to be one big family despite differences of opinion and upbringing—including the influences of their family customs. The soul mates must work together to acknowl-edge and make their families aware that they are one family. In so doing, the couple must refrain from referring to "your family" and "my family" as separate units. Instead, they must form one Circle of Love—a united whole. They will face such chal-lenges on numerous occasions. For example, whenever the two organize a get-together or celebration at their home at which both families will be present, or whenever they take vacations with other family members, they may encounter stressful situa-tions. To avoid pressures and friction, the couple must establish a solid, lasting commitment to one another.

32
RELEASE ANY DISCORD
THAT YOU MAY FEEL
TOWARD ONE ANOTHER AS
A COUPLE, AND NEVER GO TO
SLEEP ANGRY.
KISS AND MAKEUP

Never Go to Sleep Angry

When Esther and I were in the initial stages of our marriage, one of the rules that we decided to adopt was this: we promised one another that no matter how much our opinions diverged or how challenging circumstanc-es would become in the future, we would never go to sleep angry. In the heat of an argument, we would stop and realize our disagreement wasn't leading us anywhere. So, we would hold hands, embrace, thank God for one another, and kiss one another's wedding rings and makeup. We would promise to start fresh, with a new perspective in the morning, trusting in God. The following day, we would inevitably discover that our problems and difficulties had vanished into thin air, and every-thing ultimately worked out for the best. Therefore, it did not pay to worry and argue about the matter.

In our fifty-three years of marriage, we have had many dif-ferences that taught us valuable lessons; but trusting in God and the good angels saw us through every setback and led us to the best outcomes. We also came to understand the impor-tance of employing various strategies and techniques to avoid unfavorable emotions and discord. This meant setting our own rules without bringing in the influences of our backgrounds, creating our own customs, or preconceived notions about any given subject. Disagreements and anger only lead to negative emotions that are very damaging to the Circle of Love.

**33
MUTUAL RESPECT AND
APPROPIATE LANGUAGE
SHOULD ALWAYS BE
USED IN FRONT OF
THE CHILDREN, FAMILY,
AND FRIENDS**

We must practice love and patience, try to accept one another, talk without arguing or insulting each other or our family members, learn to compromise and share moments of passion and affection as a couple and with our family. By doing so, we will create memories that last a lifetime.

We must also balance our wants and needs, pray and meditate each day to receive God's energy together. These practices create a climate of love, harmony, peace, and prosperity.

Never Speak Negatively About Your Mate

Early on, we learned that if we have nothing good to say, say nothing. It's best not to contradict one another in front of the children, family, or friends—even in jest. Everyone who surrounds the couple must always know that the two are one unit, with one purpose: to serve God and complete their mission and that they are each other's. Their children, family, friends, co-workers, or boss often try to persuade them to make decisions without consulting their spouse. Most of the time, their core reason for doing so is to test their loyalty and commitment to practice their convic-tions. If these tests influence the couple in any way, they can generate discord and dissatisfaction in the marital relationship.

There have been times when we speak inappropriately about our spouse in front of other people, family, and friends, such as telling jokes or making comments that tend to cause our spouse to feel uneasy and even embarrassed. These statements come from media influences that constantly encourage this type of conversation, but the marital relationship suffers. One essential practice in a marriage is to refrain from contradicting one another—for example, when both partners have different versions of the same story, and one spouse jumps in to contradict the other, this can cause disharmony between the two. Many times, those who are listening are entertained by the bickering and fuel the conversation just for the sake of amusement.

In other cases, parenting styles may conflict, and one parent may interfere and demoralize the other in front of the children (in the case of disciplinary measures, for example). Not sur-prisingly, an argument can break out in front of the children as a result. To avoid such unpleasantness, if one parent rep-rimands a child, the other spouse should step in and defend their partner's position, even if there is a difference of opinion. When opinions are at odds, the couple should wait to discuss the matter in private and devise a mutually beneficial means of handling similar circumstances in the future. The couple must never demonstrate division between them in front of anyone but rather operate as a unified whole.

34
**CONFLICTS OF OPINION
SHOULD NOT CAUSE
ARGUMENTATION.
ALWAYS TRY TO REACH
A COMPROMISE**

It's About "WE," NOT "I"

The couple must always act as a unified whole—as "we," not "I." When both consciously decide to relinquish their "single" status and become a couple, they should always refer to themselves as a single entity. When a family member or friend asks them about a matter or invites them to join in special occasions, mutual consultation is always the first order of the day. Be firm in this practice to preserve the marital bond. Spousal communication is also vital when dealing with the couple's parents, who sometimes may try to orchestrate the decision-making processes or influence domestic, business, or financial outcomes. Some may want to interfere and insist that the matter at hand be addressed according to their expecta-tions and perspectives, even if the other spouse disagrees. The spouse whose parents want to provide such advice must be very diplomatic and explain that although their offer of help is deeply appreciated and will be taken into consideration, the couple prefers to make decisions together in their Circle of Love. It's best to say something like, "I will present your suggestion to my spouse, and if we agree, we will follow through; but if not, we must allow God to guide us in the right direction."

The "WE-NOT-I" mindset is the key to a happy marriage.

35
PRACTICE TOLERANCE, PATIENCE, AND MUTUAL UNDERSTANDING TO CREATE A HARMONIOUS AND PEACEFUL HOME-LIFE

Mutually Agree on Financial Matters

Early in our marriage, my father taught me how to create a budgeting system that helps maintain proper control over our finances. When we got married, our salaries were meager, and if my father had not instructed us to budget our money, we would not have been able to manage. Even though our salaries are larger today, we must maintain our budgetary system to monitor our increased income and expenses. Computer programs such as QuickBooks, ™, or Spread Sheets can help us control our finances.

The budget must contain all the income that we take into our household and all our expenses. It also has a place for donations, entertainment, vacations, and emergencies. We mutually agree on how we distribute our funds and make every decision together—particularly about lending or donating money, vacation plans, and savings. When friends or family approach us and ask to borrow money, we discuss the matter and act upon it according to God's guidance. We always remember that God is the supplier of all things and wants us to administer the funds that are divinely bestowed to help those in need. Acts of love and kindness are among the most crucial factors in depurating our souls. Therefore, we must make decisions in a triangle—God, you, and me. Acting without mutual consent or in private can lead to a severe breach of trust with God and our soul mate.

Sometimes, we go through slack financial periods due to illness, loss of work, etc. At such times, we must revisit our budget and temporarily cut corners while we pray and try to supplement that income with emergency money and await God's instruction to proceed in new and better ways.

Remember that God has a purpose for everything that happens in our lives. Sometimes, when things become more challenging, God is trying to bring us to another level of awareness and un-derstanding that would never be reached without obstacles.

Household finances must be managed like a business. If our expenses exceed our budget at any time, we must review our expenditures and temporarily limit certain "luxuries," such as recreation, entertainment, vacations, etc. Borrowing money or using credit cards to temporarily subsidize the additional income needed or to take care of substantial debts (such as a mortgage) can be very helpful. God will help us make the best use of it. At the same time, when these resources are used for pure luxury or entertainment when we are in the middle of a financial test, excessive expenditures can backfire and create financial burdens. These conditions, in turn, can sometimes lead to more borrowing and cause more hardship and strain on the marriage. This is especially true when one spouse wants to control the marital finances while the other does not pay attention to the outcomes of improper decision-making.

36
COUPLES SHOULD MAKE FINANCIAL DECISIONS AS ONE ENTITY, WITHOUT BEING SWAYED BY OUTSIDE INFLUENCES

Decades years ago, we went through a devastating financial test when our garment manufacturing business burned down, and we lost all our money. We needed to pray more and act on God's promise. We had to readjust our lifestyle and look for new ways to make a living. So, we took the initiative and began to install window tinting, wallpapers, draperies, and blinds. It so happened that my wife sent in a coupon for a free course in general contracting at a local school. Although she never expected anything to come of that effort, she received word that we had won. When she told me the news, she was so excited. I thought, Well, this is a sign from God to go that route, and we will take it. So, after lots of challenges, studying, and taking the test three times, we passed and received our general contrac-tor's license. Although I was the one who took the course and the tests, I refer to both of us because my supportive wife was always at my side, helping me through that endeavor with all her heart and encouraging me for many months. After that, we received a promotion to attend a seminar on real estate and how to buy houses with little or no money down. Later, God allowed us to buy our first property, but we had no money. However, we remembered the lessons we learned in the course and decided to put our knowledge into practice. After we presented an offer and a few subsequent negotiations, the seller accepted our terms, and we used our credit card to get a cash advance to buy the property. Later on, we completed all of the necessary repairs in the duplex. We increased the rent and returned to the bank to borrow funds to pay the existing loan and withdraw some money. God granted us that opportunity, which began our entre-preneurial venture in the real estate business.

37
MAKE DECISIONS IN
A TRIANGLE:
GOD, YOU, AND YOUR PARTNER

God

You ▲ **Your Partner**

Intimacy Is Not Just Physical; It Is An Expression of Love At All Times

Sex and intimacy are natural acts that the couple should practice spontaneously but not routinely. The satisfaction of spontaneous intimacy in a marriage, with passion and the intention of pleasing our partner, is a blessing we should always cherish. The attraction for one another should be present all the time. We cannot use intimacy as a reward for the other person just because they provide what we desire or withhold intimate relations because we did not get our way. God created us to be born, grow, get married, and multiply—a solemn commandment. We should not compare our partners to the depictions of models in magazines or on television. Instead, we should always seek to compliment, validate and express words of love to one another, setting aside time to send a message that expresses our abiding appreciation and love. This type of communication can sometimes manifest as a thoughtful gift without ulterior motives. Just as displays of affection should never serve as a reward, neither should they be a substitute for an apology. Instead, they should be pure and unrelated to any wrongdoing, never prompting the other spouse to ask, "What is this for? What did you do wrong?" Through our fifty-three years of marriage, we learned that God had given us the opportunity to share love and intimacy with blessings. We believe this is the most essential part of the equation—the essence of a successful marriage. As we mentioned earlier, this type of connection doesn't just happen, like turning an electric switch on and off. It must be a mutual understanding and expression throughout the entire day, with various displays and signs of affection and love. For example, everyone needs compliments, affirmations, and praise. This is more important for the female than the male. However, This does not mean the wife does not have to compliment her husband. No, please! Let us both commit to always showing our expressions of love and praise to one another! This will increase mutual fulfillment in matters of love and intimacy. This is how God uses obstacles and tests and turns them into testimonies. When we encounter difficulties, such as health and financial issues, trusting in God and knowing that the Almighty has a purpose in our lives allows the Creator to show us a better, more profitable path.

**38
EXPRESSIONS OF LOVE
ARE NOT JUST PHYSICAL.
INTIMACY SHOULD BE
SPONTANEOUS AND FROM
THE HEART**

**39
A COUPLE'S LOVE FOR EACH OTHER
SHOULD BE A LIVING TESTAMENT TO
GOD'S BLESSINGS**

SUCCESS & PROSPERITY

Create Lasting Memories

Always create memories you will have in the palm of your hands to pull out like magicians and talk about throughout the years. I recall not knowing what to buy for Esther on our eleventh anniversary. I prayed to God, and when I was driving to work, I made a sudden STOP. When I looked at the stop sign, I had an epiphany: Ah! I said to myself. I will go to the jewelry store and design a medal in the shape of a STOP sign, inscribed with the words, 'I WILL NEVER STOP LOVING YOU,' and on the other side, it would read,

40
LOVING MEMORIES
ARE THE LIGHTS
THAT SPARKS THE FLAME
OF LOVE

'THIS IS MY ELEVENTH COMMANDMENT ON OUR ELEVENTH ANNIVERSARY.' The following year, Esther wanted to give me something we would cherish for a long time. She ordered two engraved bracelets—one with the name 'Marcos' and the other 'Esther.'

We have been wearing these tokens of love for many years. When we celebrated our fiftieth anniversary, a quote came to mind: "I AM MY BELOVED's AND MY BELOVED IS MINE." I said to Esther, "Let's exchange our bracelets. I will wear yours, and you wear mine, and we will always remember the quote. Then, when people ask about it, we

SUCCESS & PROSPERITY

can testify about the blessings that God has given us in our marriage, and we will tell them that we were fortunate to meet our soul mate—all to the Glory of God." Of course, all of these memories and hundreds more that we have created throughout our years together always help us confront life's challenges as we maintain a spirit of love between us. We still use those memories to ignite and share our love for one another.

41
SIGNS OF COMMITMENT AND LOVE GROW SIGNIFICANTLY THROUGHOUT THE YEARS. HONOR YOUR VOWS BY CREATING LASTING MEMORIES

We vividly remember a day when we entered a store, and the attendant politely posed questions to make us feel at ease. She noticed that the bracelet on my wrist said "Esther."

"Is that your name?" she asked.

"No, my name is Mordechai," I answered.

My wife displayed her bracelet inscribed with the name "Marcos."

"Why are you wearing each other's bracelets?" the attendant inquired.

"We have been wearing these for over forty years, but when we celebrated our 50th anniversary, we decided that as a sign of commitment and blessings to one another, we would exchange bracelets and wear each other's."

"That is so beautiful and reminds me of my husband's commitment to me. Every week, he would give me a dollar as a token of his commitment and how much I mean to him, and he would increase the offering by one dollar every year (That is, he would give me two, three, four dollars, etc. in each successive year of marriage). We just celebrated our forty-sixth anniver-sary, and he has remained faithful to that promise. I love it! Of course, it's not the money that matters, but the beauty of our commitment and the love he expresses to me every week."

**42
BY TRUSTING IN GOD.
WE WILL ACHIEVE
BALANCE AND ALLOW
BLESSINGS AND PEACE
TO FOLLOW**

We were very impressed by the woman's testimony and wished her a life filled with peace, love, health, blessings, and prosperity.

Balance Your Spiritual Income and Expenditures On Your Life's Balance Sheet

In the same way that business-es must have good record-keeping of income, expenses, and operation, along with a well-organized balance sheet (which is a barometer of how the business functions), we need to have good record-keeping in our marriage, as well as in our individual

SUCCESS & PROSPERITY

lives, to proceed and prosper. In this way, we can receive and give love, peace, and eternal life.

Income is represented by the faith we maintain in God throughout the day and our actions throughout our lives when confronted with every test the Creator presents. We amass spiritual points in the income column by doing charitable deeds and acts of love and kindness, showing mercy and understand-ing of our soul mate and family. We must avoid complaining about everyone's actions and behaviors and always express compliments, encouragement, love, positivity, and understand-ing. Adhering to these daily practices will increase our points in the income column since we exemplify goodness in the lives of our partner, family, and friends. That is what God wants from each one of us.

Let us use an example to illustrate our point. It can be as simple as looking for an item we have misplaced and cannot find. We start looking and ask our mate for help. As time passes, and we cannot find the item, we may become anxious and upset and even blame our partner for our state of mind. The more we remain in this state of anxiety, the more we expend unnecessary energy and emotion, and those attitudes will add points to the expense column.

Let us look at the same example in a positive light.

When we are connected with God- energy, we should be able to control our emotions and rely on God's presence, which provides us with wisdom, calmness, and peace to bring hope to our partner or family member, showing them that we are living a life of faith. God will always help us with everything, including petty things like misplacing something. Therefore, let us be calm and allow God to work. When we are at peace and rest all our trust in the Creator, we realize that God will show us the way, and we will find what was missing. Always remember that there is a purpose and a reason for everything in our lives. As soon as we acknowledge God in all we do and have faith that God is in control, everything will come to light, and the item will appear where we least expected. These practices will enable us to triumph over our tests and grant us victory.

Similarly, when we run a business, all we accomplish daily impacts the income or expenditure column. In turn, the income and expenses columns will affect our assets, liabilities, and balance sheet, reflecting whether the business is functioning well. In like manner, our spiritual books have an income and expenditure column, which monitors how we behave toward our spouse, family, and friends, and a balance sheet that tracks the spiritual health we maintain in our life. Just as businesses sometimes lose money and fold, many people are spiritually bankrupt because they do not accept that we must live a life of faith in God. It is the only way that we can find meaning. Therefore, we must live according to God's principles so that we can grow, prosper, maintain our health, proceed in the direction of our mission, fulfill the goals that the Creator has ordained, and at the end of our mission, achieve eternal peace in the world to come. It is never too late to start today if we have not done so before. It is vital to acknowledge problems that arise in various ways, such as with marriage, health, finances, family setbacks, etc., which are God's signs and tests intended to challenge us, correct our wrongdoings, and achieve the purpose for which we were born.

A few weeks ago, we attended a gathering with friends and family from our temple. We were sitting in the dining room, having lunch, when one of our dear friends asked us how our book was coming along.

"We're doing well," I replied.

"Can you explain the message you are trying to communicate to your readers?" she asked.

"Gladly," I responded. "The book is about motivation, in-spiration, spirituality, finding our soul mate, and completing our mission according to God's will to achieve eternal life. Therefore, the day that our spirits are called to return to God, we will rejoice in eternal peace in paradise."

SUCCESS & PROSPERITY

On this journey called life, tread the path toward
Divine intervention.
Do it God's Way.

"Can you elaborate more about soul mates?" our friend inquired.

My wife answered, "Of course. Go ahead, Mordechai. Explain what we have written about finding a soul mate."

"Esther and I feel very privileged that God allowed us to meet one another—each other's soul mates—at a very early age by taking us to different places in the world, only to land in New York and meet one another, fall in love, raise our family, and serve our Creator," I began.

"What are the criteria for identifying your soul mate?" she asked.

"That is an excellent question. In Chapter 3, the reader will find the answer," I replied.

"Can you share a few of them?"

"The essential requirements are faith in God, belief, patience, and waiting for the appropriate signs.

At that moment, a gentleman across the table from us joined the conversation and inquired, "Does that mean that non-believ-ers don't have an opportunity to have a good life, find a compat-ible partner, and be prosperous?"

I said, "That is a very good point. No, not everyone in this world believes in God or eternal life, which is precisely why God has inspired us to write our book—to demonstrate, in layperson's terms, the importance of living a fulfilling life. The Master of the Universe guided and showed us the way."

The man interrupted me and replied, "Well, neither my wife nor I believe in God, and we have been happily married for fifty-two years."

I answered, "Good for you. When you complete your life here, do you believe you will have eternal life?"

"No," the man affirmed. "If I do not believe in God or pray, why should I believe in eternal life? I will be dead when I die, and there is nothing else we can do about it."

I looked at the man earnestly. "You know, God gives us the free will to think that way also, but sooner or later, we should find the truth."

43
BELIEVERS AND NON-BELIEVERS CAN CO-EXIST IN THE WORLD. WE ARE ALL ON THIS JOURNEY TOGETHER

He changed the conversation to another subject, and Esther signaled me to go for coffee. Sometimes, things are better left unsaid, especially when discussions reach an impasse.

As a reader, you can either be inspired by the positive affir-mations we share in this book and begin to experience favorable changes in your life, or you can feel a disconnect from God and continue to live your life according to your own perspectives. The choice belongs to each of us, and God does not compel us to worship or accept the Divine Presence.

I encourage everyone reading these pages to begin to live a life of faith in God with your soul mate so that both of you can mutually create a Circle of Love and grow in faith to share with your families and friends. Allow your lives to be guided by the spirit of God so that you can control your material impulses, speak only positively, freely give compliments, and refrain from any actions or behaviors that may cause a disturbance in your life and family.

Below we offer to find sixteen affirmations that all of us should recite together to remind ourselves of our commitment to one another in the presence of God in our lives.

44
BESTOW FAITH WHERE THERE IS DOUBT,
BESTOW LOVE WHERE HATE IS PRESENT,
BESTOW UNDERSTANDING WHERE THERE IS INDIFFERENCE,
BESTOW ACCEPTANCE WHERE THERE IS REJECTION,
BESTOW PARDON WHERE THERE ARE CONFLICTS,
BESTOW BLESSINGS WHERE THERE IS ILL WILL

AFFIRMATION TO BE RECITED BY AND FOR SOUL MATES

(1) Every morning, we will praise and glorify God together.

(2) We thank God with all our heart and soul for everything we have.

(3) We understand that God created each one of us in different circles of our lives to bring us together to form our own Circle of Love, to be fruitful, and multiply.

(4) We believe that when we decided to join our lives together, we were following God's plan for our good.

(5) We believe the promise God gave us: we will never walk alone in this world.

(6) We believe that I AM MY BELOVED'S AND MY BELOVED IS MINE.

(7) We believe that throughout time, both our families have united as one big family.

(8) We believe that we have different souls, characters, and backgrounds.

(9) We should make our own rules about how to communicate with each other. We will never go to sleep angry with each other. Instead, we will kiss and make up.

(10) We will never comment negatively about our partner in front of our children, family, or friends—even in the form of a joke.

(11) We will respect each other and always speak words of love, encourage, and compliment each other to create lasting lifetime memories—here and in the world to come.

(12) We will manage our financial decisions together and proceed according to our budget, so as not to impose economic burdens on our Circle of Love.

(13) We will never use intimacy as either a penalty or a manipulative tool for personal gain.

(14) We will strive for respect, understanding, love, passion, and affection all the days of our lives.

(15) In everything we say and do, we will always refer to "we," not "I." As a couple, we are a united whole.

(16) We will always make time to be together, so that our memories will last forever. Life is beautiful and filled with blessings—no matter what phase of life we enter. Together, we will enjoy our journey on earth and into eternity.

To Say "I Love You"

The depth of love can be shown in three little words, "I love you"—words so simple, yet profound and everlasting.

To say "I love you" forms a heart-connection with your soul mate, shared between only two—a display of romance, compassion, and trust.

To say "I love you" means "I see you, I understand and appreciate who you are."

To say "I love you" signifies "I chose you as my soul mate, above and to the exclusion of all others, as my partner in life and for all time."

To say "I love you" means that God destined us to be a unified whole, individuals in our opinions and approaches to life, but one in love, faith and respect.

Such powerful words, spoken as a covenant of our soul-bond that cannot ever be severed, enduring for eternity.

CHAPTER 4

DOING IT GOD'S WAY

All human beings have decision-making abilities that give us a specific direction in life. On the day of our birth, God introduces the spirit of life into our bodies and provides us with the ability to learn, have faith in the Almighty, attain knowledge, give and receive love and mercy, and the capacity to understand good and evil. As we grow and learn, God allows us to make choices that enable us to navigate our lives into various ports. Each decision inevitably produces different results, either good or bad, and each choice will either direct us away from our mission or bring us closer to the path of prosperity, health, love, happiness, peace, and spiritual growth.

On the journey, we must define the nature of our mission in life and what we want to do with the talents that God has given us. To accomplish this goal, we must recognize that God is our Creator and eternal parent, waiting with open arms to help us fulfill our mission and provide abundance in all things, along with the peace, love, and prosperity we require to fulfill our mission.

45
BE A FORCE FOR GOOD IN THE WORLD TO COUNTERACT FORCES OF EVIL, ILL WILL, AND INDIFFERENCE

We must decide whether we want to achieve our objectives our way, with our own resources (and therefore, learn the hard way), or to do things God's way and reap all the benefits that our Creator provides us. We may face different trials, tribula-tions, and suffering, for which we sometimes blame God, but these tests result from prior mistakes, including those we made in our previous life. God allowed them to happen because we attempted to accomplish everything through our own wisdom without involving or consulting our Ultimate Source of Creation in decision-making. We can compare this to a lack of trust in authority figures, such as team coaches, teachers, parents, doctors, or other people in positions of prominence, endowed with the ability to guide us on the right path. Doing things our way seems to be a trend in the world today, creating the illusion that we can do everything independently, but in truth, making decisions without consulting others—and God, in particular—leads us down a road of disharmony and stagnation.

If we want to be successful and happy, fulfill our dreams and career goals, and have peace of mind and abundance in this world while preparing to receive our reward in the world to come when our mission on earth has been fulfilled, we must follow the examples of other successful people who came before us and emulate their behavior. Before making any decisions, successful people consult with experts in their field of interest, research the subject, and analyze the advice presented to them. If they accept God as their ultimate guide and protector, they will pray on that decision (which will be revealed to them in many different forms). Alternatively, if they have the wisdom to be open to the signs available to them, they may listen to the little voice inside that steers them in the right direction. Simply stated, that is the definition of "doing it God's way." It is important to remember that everything in this world is a test, and when we recognize that fact and do everything God's way, we understand that ev-erything has a purpose and a reason.

46
ALLOW GOD TO BE YOUR ETERNAL GUIDING COMPASS THAT LEADS YOU TO THE FULFILLMENT OF YOUR MISSION

Tribulations may exist as life lessons, growth experiences, or sources of enlightenment. God gives us the opportunity to correct the mistakes that we have made with our previous choices. Therefore, whenever we are confronted with unpleas-ant or trying situations, we must remember that we are only being tested. With God's help and a positive attitude in every-thing we do, we will be victorious. When a resolution to our problems seems to escape us, we must not allow fear or doubt to take root in our minds, and we must not declare defeat. When we give in to negative thoughts, fear, self-pity, disappointment, and despair, we inevitably experience setbacks. To overcome these obstacles, we must allow God to take control. By talking to our Creator, presenting all our travails with sincerity while recog-nizing our mistakes and repenting, we will transform negative thoughts into affirmation and victory—as if what we desire has already happened. That is where faith and living in gratitude come into play. When we reach that point of understanding, we can declare victory over our challenges—even when outward signs point to an adverse outcome.

47
GOD HAS A PURPOSE AND A REASON FOR EVERYTHING. TESTS ARE THE BUILDING BLOCKS OF VICTORY

Often, we cannot understand God's signs in the limited framework of our human minds. Nonetheless, we must ac-knowledge that God is in control and the Almighty's actions have inherent meaning, apart from our understanding. When we place our trust and faith in God, the Creator will guide us on the right path toward ultimate fulfillment, healing, and success.

When we elect to do things God's way, everything naturally flows and turns out for the best. When we allow our bodies to assume control of our spirits, mistakes, troubles, setbacks, and many other negative consequences follow in succession. Even if we feel that we are on track and having fun, experiencing pros-perity, or advancing in our careers or relationships, our spiritual awareness tends to decline, and our mission's fulfillment is placed on hold.

It is important to know that God is always there, prepared, and willing to help, sending us messages and signs to guide us on the right path and confront life's tests, whether these are physical, psychological, emotional, financial, or related to inter-personal relationships. No matter what we are going through, we call upon God to forgive us for trying to do things our way, and we repent and listen to the inner whispers of our hearts (God's voice). This will trigger Divine intervention, and God will help us mend the error of our ways, provide the proper resources, and set us on the right course to complete our mission victoriously.

As we go about our mission, the question becomes, "How do I know I am DOING IT GOD'S WAY?" The answer lies in our choice to listen to the spirit rather than the inclinations of the flesh. The body tends to lead us toward the material world without regard for the consequences of the spirit's ultimate path and destination.

48
CHOOSING TO DO
THINGS GOD'S WAY
MEANS CONSCIOUSLY
SURRENDERING TO
A GREATER WISDOM
THAN OUR LIMITED
HUMAN UNDERSTANDING

The spiritual journey is the reason we are born into this world. The spirit is eternal, unburdened by materialistic concerns because it knows God is the provider of everything. Abundance will be ours when we focus on the mission God has prepared. The spirit is the conduit that intercepts the material world and allows us to acknowledge and communicate with God, the ultimate Source and Prime Mover of life. When we are present and in tune with the Creator, we sense we are "DOING IT GOD'S WAY." Everything will start falling into place, we will encounter peace in everything, abundance and success will begin to flow, and our lives will become more meaningful in every respect.

God's path is paved with the wisdom, prosperity, peace, love, success, and abundance we require to live a fulfilling life without focusing solely on material, mundane concerns. Walking the road GOD'S WAY also reminds us of the most important reason for our existence: to fulfill our spiritual mission. We must remember that our presence on earth is a direct result of our choices before birth to come to earth in a specific incarna-tion with a preassigned, agreed -upon mission. Of course, our path will have stumbling blocks and obstacles, but God will ul-timately lead us to victory if we follow the Divine will.

Victory is also a test of our unique characters – our ability to give glory and gratitude unto God and credit those who deserve recognition or our tendency to blame God or others for our failures. An attitude of gratitude is always a sign that we are on the path to DOING IT GOD'S WAY, equipped with the under-standing that God is our ultimate guide and source of sustenance on our journey. This includes acknowledging the existence of God's many angels and methods of providing us with the as-sistance that we need.

49
WHEN WE ARE PRESENT AND IN TUNE WITH THE CREATOR, WE KNOW THAT WE ARE "DOING IT GOD'S WAY"

We have learned throughout our lives to show our gratitude to God. These examples may be helpful to our readers and inspire them to perform acts of love and kindness with gratitude to God so that they can take their journey toward a successful destina-tion and a life of abundance and fulfillment. Naturally, there is nothing new under the sun, but our suggestions are intended to set vital concepts for prosperity before our readers' eyes—ev-erything that is everyone's inherent right to claim through faith in God.

The Two- Dollar Certificate

In keeping with our mission to perpetuate acts of kindness, we give out a two-dollar bill to anyone whom God places in our path, whose kindness and love are worthy of acknowledgment in the form of a "Certificate of Recognition of Acts of Love and Kindness—When people receive our gesture, they are encour-aged and inspired to act and continue the trend of spreading love and joy to others—not just because they receive the two-dollar certificate, but also because the act of giving signifies gratitude to God. This small gesture of goodwill demonstrates that goodness and hope can be represented in many forms, sometimes the least of which proves to be the most powerful.

SUCCESS & PROSPERITY

One day, a dear friend of mine, born in Israel, informed me that the Hebrew word "Natan," meaning "to give," is a palin-drome—it reads the same backward and forward, from right to left and left to right. My friend explained the lesson he learned from his mother: Every time you give with honorable intention, you receive much more because you are doing God's will.

We continue spreading the work of God. As messengers of God, we are committed to perpetuating acts of love and kindness. We tell everyone that with the certificate of recognition, God has inspired us to motivate others to do the same, bringing good fortune to themselves and their families. Love and goodness have a domino effect and are cyclical—part of the cycle of life.

We have witnessed many testimonies of how God has worked in the lives of many recipients of the two-dollar cer-tificate—too many to enumerate here —but God has provided the most remarkable testimonies to us. Since we started sharing the two-dollar bill as a blessing to others, God has blessed us in many ways and has brought us prosperity. Most importantly, it has helped us share God's love with others by giving a positive testimony of love and prosperity.

50
STRUCTURING OUR LIVES
AROUND GRATITUDE TO GOD
SHOWS US THE PATH
TO ABUNDANCE

51
**EVERY TIME YOU GIVE
WITH HONORABLE INTENTION
YOU RECEIVE MUCH MORE
BECAUSE YOU ARE
DOING GOD'S WILL**

The Dollar Torah

A couple of years later, we had an opportunity to receive an origami of a one-dollar bill, converted into the symbol of a Torah (the Old Testament). We asked Aly, the person who made it for us, to teach us how to make the origami dollar Torah.

Aly instructed Mordechai, "Raise your right hand and promise God that you will use this origami of the Torah dollar any time someone is celebrating a special occasion of any kind,"

We have been very loyal to that promise and have given many Torah dollars to people celebrating various occasions or events, adding something significant to us. After crafting it, we provide the recipient with the Priesthood Blessing.

We also acknowledge that in so doing, we infuse the idea of sharing acts of love, kindness, and goodwill in the minds of others. No act, just like no individual, exists in isolation. We are all part of an interconnected chain of humanity, each deserving a cheer and recognition, all to the glory of God.

The AY-YA-YA-YA-YAI Cheer

Another symbolic representation of gratitude that we adopted after a trip to Israel is the AY-YA-YA-YA-YAI cheer. In a gesture of gratitude to anyone—family members, friends, the congregation, or anyone God inspires us to cheer in the Creator's name, we repeat that individual's name three times and then shout, "AY-YA-YA-YA-YAI," moving our hands in the air, from one side to the other, and finally pouring out blessings to them with a movement of our fingers, signifying that we are sprinkling goodness and prosperity upon them in the name of God. This example does not require any investment of money. We just have to be willing to look for opportunities to pour blessings upon others and to share acts of love, kindness, and goodwill.

52
WE ARE ALL PART OF AN
INTERCONNECTED CHAIN OF HUMANITY.
IT IS IMPORTANT TO
CHEER AND UPLIFT OTHERS –
ALL TO THE GLORY OF GOD

Thank you, God! It is great to sense and know that we are living our lives your way!

Adhering to the following practices will enable you to live a God-filled life—God's way:

- Begin each day by giving thanks to God;
- Pray and listen for answers—the whispers of your inner voice;
- Ask for forgiveness. If you make a mistake, repent and correct it;
- If something does not bring you inner peace, refrain from doing it;
- Love and respect yourself and everyone around you;
- Show love and kindness in everything you do;
- Be persistent and steadfast with everything that God reveals that you should do;
- Follow your dreams;
- Learn how to say "no" to things that are wrong for you and others;
- Take care of the body that God has given you;
- Seek out those things that are in your best interests;
- If something goes wrong, believe that if God allowed that event or circumstance to occur, it was for your ultimate best. You may not understand God's reasoning immediately, but remember that everything happens for a purpose. Look for the message and opportunity God wants you to learn from your challenges. Sometimes, shared pain heals wounds. Reach out and allow yourself to assist and be helped, in turn;
- Believe that God has a purpose for everything;
- Never give up, no matter how difficult the circumstances are;
- Trust that God is going to grant you victories;
- Always bestow honor and glory unto God in all things;
- Say "Amen" when you hear someone saying something positive or an inspirational prayer by affirming that it will come to pass. When we say "Amen," both the giver and the receiver reap the benefit.

In the following chapters, these suggested practices will be integrated into the life lessons we wish to share, all of which have been inspired by our Creator.

SUCCESS & PROSPERITY

By holding this book in hand, our readers are taking the first step on their journey toward success and living a fulfilled life, with the opportunity to declare, "I DID IT GOD'S WAY."

53
HAVE PATIENCE AND TRUST IN DIVINE TIMING, WHICH IS INFINITE, RATHER THAN VIEWING LIFE FROM OUR LIMITED PERSPECTIVE

54
WE CAN OBTAIN EVERYTHING THAT WE DESIRE AS LONG AS WE DO IT GOD'S WAY, HAVE PATIENCE, AND REST ON GOD'S TIME

Lessons to Treasure from "Doing It God's Way"

In the process, trust is an essential element. That is, we cannot merely say that we will relinquish control if, when doing so, we do not place our complete trust and faith in God. The beauty of doing this involves the understanding that we, as mere mortals, are limited in our abilities and perceptions, the outcomes we seek will necessarily be imperfect if we do not offer up control to our Creator.

Our view of the passage of days, hours, minutes, and moments is also finite in our space and time. We measure time in the very static confines of our limited understanding, but God's comprehension of time is far more expansive. It is infinite. Therefore, if what we desire to happen does not occur in our narrow framework, we need not be discouraged because God's time is unending. If we think of time in this respect, we have all the time in the world to accomplish that which involves com-pleting our mission. We must communicate our wants and needs to God, our best friend, who always walks beside us, presenting opportunities, putting the right people in our path, counseling, and guiding us all the way. The Creator may not be visible or within the realm of our five senses, but the Presence is always there.

Along the way, patience is of the essence. Sometimes, it is difficult for human beings to experience what we perceive to be the slow progression of things. The reason is that we are always looking at clocks and watches, believing that they govern time. God, however, is the ultimate timekeeper, despite our conven-tional notions of hours, days, etc.

Patience sometimes requires retreating in prayer and medita-tion, giving thanks to God for all the gifts in our lives—even those that have not yet taken shape. It's important to remember that even though we cannot see results immediately or within the timeframe we believe they will happen, that does not mean that they are not in the making—just as a butterfly emerges from its chrysalis as a tiny caterpillar. This is a painful and often drawn-out process involving enormous struggle

SUCCESS & PROSPERITY

until, at last, a triumphant butterfly emerges, ready to spread its wings. Any form of creation—even the formation of an idea—takes time to materialize. However, if we sit quietly and with confidence, knowing that the manifestation of what we desire is imminent and in the hands of the ultimate Intelligent Artist, we will be able to withstand what we sometimes consider to be "the long haul."

Inevitably, the answers will come—perhaps, not by our measurements and calculations of time, but rather, in the Grand Scheme. Let's trust and DO IT GOD'S WAY; the victories, successes, healings, promotions, breakthroughs, and all forms of happiness will be ours.

55
KINDNESS IS INFECTOUS.
THE MORE WE GIVE, THE
MORE WE RECEIVE.
AS A RESULT, WE WITNESS
THE FRUITS OF OUR
GIVING REFLECTED IN
THE WORLD AROUND US,
MANIFESTING A TRUE
REPRESENTATION OF GOD

CHAPTER 5

DECISION-MAKING THROUGH DIVINE CONSULTATION

56
WALKING THE ROAD GOD'S WAY ALSO REMINDS US OF THE MOST IMPORTANT REASON FOR OUR EXISTENCE: TO FULFILL OUR SPIRITUAL MISSION

As discussed in the last chapter, trying to act independently and without Divine Intervention leads us astray. We may ask, "If God is always present in our lives, why must we pause in our daily routine to consult the Ultimate Source? The reason is that every decision impacts our usual practices and will also have eternal repercussions. Since God dwells in the realm of spirit, it is essential to consult with the Almighty before taking affirmative steps in the direction of our choice. As mentioned earlier, God communicates with us in various forms to guide us on the road to happiness, peace, and prosperity.

We may ask questions concerning our health, business prospects, college decisions, and other concerns, such as the vehicle we should purchase. Nothing is trivial or unimportant in God's eyes. Decisions are based on various factors that involve unique circumstances in an individual's life.

Another element that informs the decision-making process is marital status. For example, single people exercise their de-cision-making abilities differently than married couples. In the case of the latter group, mutual understanding and communica-tion are critical ingredients for happiness and successful deci-sion-making. For fifty-nine years of married life, my wife and I routinely communicate openly and consult with one another whenever we must make a decision that could affect us in one way or another. In addition to exchanging bracelets, we occasionally wear matching outfits to emphasize our sense of unity.

57
CONSULTATION WITH GOD
IS THE FIRST CRITICAL STEP
IN THE DECISION-MAKING
PROCESS

Compromise is also an essential component of the process, whether we decide what we will eat for dinner, what type of vacation we want to take, how we want to allocate our resources, or what charity we wish to help. We perpetuate our joy and harmony as a couple and individuals by arriving at mutually beneficial, satisfactory conclusions.

Similarly, those who act alone must consider that their decisions will have a ripple effect on their finances, happiness, health, prosperity, and spiritual outcome, along with those who are part of their circle of life. None of us is an island, and every one of our decisions can impact others – even those we have never met.

No matter how and under what circumstances we engage in our decision-making capacities among ourselves, our primary focus must be on God's guidance and divine wisdom. The question becomes, "If God has specific plans for us that we are unaware of and don't understand the signs that God provides us, how can we achieve or obtain what we most desire?" The answer is: If what we desire is in accordance with the mission that God has given us and is in line with the divine plan, God will provide us with signs to show us the correct path. Most important, peace will come upon us. If our desires contradict our mission, we do not want to take the time to consult God in prayer, and we fail to wait for the signs that God provides to show us our mistakes. If we discover that the outcome is not what we anticipated, we must accept that we have made a wrong decision by not asking our Creator for assistance. God will use the outcome to help us understand that the Creator has a purpose in every aspect of our lives. We will realize that keeping God out of the decision-making process will cause harm, but if we call upon the Creator to guide and direct us, we will experience a victory. Let us not forget that what we do in this life will ulti-mately affect our eternal lives.

58
JOINT DECISION-MAKING AND MUTUAL ACCORD ARE ESSENTIAL IN EVERY MARRIAGE

One of the most essential resources that God gives us is the ability to access inner peace, to maintain consistent divine com-munication. The doors to our souls should always remain open. Just as the "inner whispers" speak to us in various ways, so does the voice of inner peace. Essentially, the alignment of body and spirit provides direction and clarity in our lives.

In my personal experience, I learned to pay heed to the inner voice that guided the course of our lives. The messages are always so powerful to this day, and I would like to share two significant examples with you now.

One day, while attending the funeral of our loving Uncle Enrique (Aunt Sarita's husband), I stood outside the tent under a shaded tree for sun protection. Suddenly, I heard a very clear voice speaking a vital message: "You and Esther should return to your roots and worship in the Jewish Temple. That is where you belong, where God wants you to testify about your faith and learn more."

I began to look around to see if anyone was speaking to me, but no one was there. At that moment, I realized that the message came from within my spirit.

When the burial ceremony ended and we drove back, I told Esther what had happened and the message I had received. "What do you think?" I asked. Esther replied, "I think that is a great revelation God has given you."

When everyone returned to the mourners' house, I shared the experience with Esther's mother, Lea. She embraced both of us and said, "A very good thing happened, even in this time of mourning. This is quite a testimony." Lea gave thanks to God. Later, we prayed and received the answer that we required to guide us in the right direction. Inner peace came over us, and we realized our decision was according to God's will.

Another thought came to me just recently about the battle between the earthly body and the spirit. Everything in this world is a process that begins from the time of our birth. God infuses the Spirit of Life into us with a purpose and a mission. Our spirit is connected directly with God, so God is present in every person and everywhere. God is also the Creator of our bodies. The human body has inclinations, challenges, desires, and needs and automatically responds to our subconscious minds through repetitive actions and desires. These actions are computed and embedded in our subconscious even when we don't pay attention. Our subconscious reminds us that we are hungry and controls such impulses as scratching our nose, touching our hair, and many other actions without consciously acknowledging them.

Similarly, our spirits have a mission to complete and a purpose God has provided us. We are in a constant battle between the earthly body and the spirit essence that constantly duel inside us. All of us are guided and motivated by the earthly body. Eventually, however, through unfortunate circumstances, tragic events, or at the end of our lives, we realize that we have allowed our lives to be governed by the wrong mechanism (i.e., the subconscious mind rather than the spirit).

In reflecting upon these extraordinary revelations, I seized the opportunity to continue my mission and help myself and others to grow in faith, perseverance, love, and kindness. Each of us has the ability and potential to achieve enormous heights, and this will only happen if we seek and pursue the purpose God has instilled in us through Divine Consultation and listening to our inner voice.

Through our faith, God will direct us in many ways. By acknowledging that everything in our lives works for our good, we will achieve our goals and even find answers to our questions. Therefore, we will be divinely guided to make the right decisions that will enhance our earthly lives and spirits in the hereafter.

People often wonder whether their prayers will be heard and answered. God will give us the answers in the decision -making process in many ways, either in the form of dreams, through media input, family or friend communications, and we will say, "YES! Thank you, God. I know that this is what you want me to do" (whatever the issue may be).

By acknowledging that God is working for our good in every aspect of our lives, we will be able to acquire the necessary patience and trust in God for answers to materialize. We will be delighted to see that God's divine guidance will help us to achieve our goals and receive material abundance. Then, in the hereafter, our spirits will also be glorified.

What if silence is the answer? How can we engage in divine consultation if God is speechless? The truth is that God always has answers for each of us, regardless of our religious affili-ation. Sometimes, God tests our faith and waits for the right person or circumstance to guide us. If we lose our patience and faith, we will make decisions that will bring about a negative or wrong outcome.

> **59**
> GOD WILL USE THE OUTCOME OF OUR DECISIONS TO DEMOSTRATE THAT THERE IS A DIVINE PURPOSE IN EVERY ASPECT OF OUR LIVES

Lessons of the Heart: Consulting God to Help Us Make Proper Decisions

If we only open our spiritual ears to listen and our spiritual eyes to see, we will be aligned in body and spirit. Maybe we won't like the answers, especially if they appear contrary to our desires or wishes. Sometimes, what we want to do and the decisions we must confront are unsuitable. For example, getting that job or taking that promotion might prevent us from ful-filling an even higher purpose yet to be revealed. The answers occur in God's time, which has nothing to do with our calcula-tion of earthly minutes, hours, days, or years. We will receive victory if we believe God will provide us with the right ideas or contacts to make the proper decision.

Divine consultation involves accepting what is—not what could be—while surrendering to God as the ultimate influence for our benefit. Once we take independent steps toward fulfill-ing our goals, God will take care of the rest. Therefore, even if we don't understand why things are happening at present, we must remember that God is always working for our good.

SUCCESS & PROSPERITY

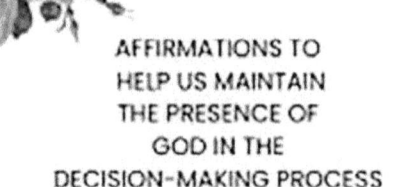

AFFIRMATIONS TO HELP US MAINTAIN THE PRESENCE OF GOD IN THE DECISION-MAKING PROCESS

When I wake up in the morning, I will give thanks to God.

I will ask God to be present in all the things I need to do today.

I will recognize that everything that will happen today will be for my good.

I will acknowledge that God has a purpose, a reason, and a plan for me today.

I will be happy and satisfied throughout the entire day.

I will face all my challenges, knowing that God will be with me all the time.

I will pray to affirm God's presence whenever fear, worry, or doubt enter my mind.

I will believe that where God is, darkness, fear, and worry will dissipate.

I am grateful for all the victories and blessings God grants me today.

AMEN, AMEN!

CHAPTER 6

ANGELS IN OUR MIDST

60
WHAT WE DO IN THIS LIFE
WILL ULTIMATELY AFFECT OUR
ETERNAL LIVES

We have been blessed to experience many signs and manifestations of answers to our prayers. Some of these have appeared as angels to assist us through the various phases of our lives and lighten our burdens. Sometimes these messengers of goodwill come to us in various forms and the most unusual places. The following are deeply personal en-counters with other-worldly forces – messengers of God that have appeared to teach us how to forge ahead affirmatively and in grace and provide validation of our goals and aspirations.

SUCCESS & PROSPERITY

One of our most significant experiences occurred when an angel appeared before us on a flight to Las Vegas. It was the summer of 1997, and we were flying from Fort Lauderdale, Florida. At the time, we were in the apartment rental business in South Florida, and two years prior, we had purchased three buildings with a mortgage and a note from the seller due in June 1997. To refinish the property, we applied to several banks but were denied. Nonetheless, we never ceased praying to God to grant us victory.

At the beginning of April, we presented our refinancing proposal to a new bank, and after meeting with the appraiser and underwriter, we felt very confident that everything was going according to plan. If our refinancing option fell through, we ran the risk of losing our investment, in addition to all the work we had done over two years to make the property thrive and succeed. Each day, we expressed gratitude to God and patiently waited for mercy.

No matter how hard we tried, the investor repeatedly denied our requests for an extension of the mortgage. "Unfortunately, you cannot refinance and turn these properties around. Therefore, I will have to claim them from you," he said authoritatively.

61
AT TIMES, HUMANS REQUIRE A BIT OF NUDGING AND INSPIRATION THAT COMES TO US IN THE FORM OF ANGELS

"We truly believe that God is testing our faith to strengthen us. God would not have made us endure this hardship if we were not going to be ultimately victorious," we insisted. "We have complete faith and trust in God's will and mercy."

Meanwhile, we were invited to Las Vegas for an apartment building expo in May but were reluctant to travel amid the re-financing venture's pressures. A call to the banker, however, solidified our intentions. "I'm still awaiting approval from the board. I will keep in touch, and you can also call me from Las Vegas," he said. We were elated, knowing that we were being divinely guided.

With so many preoccupations diverting our attention, we were simultaneously preparing for our B'nai Mitzvah ceremony—a ritual in the Jewish faith that typically occurs when a young man of thirteen or a young lady of twelve transitions into adulthood. Esther intuitively felt that her upcoming birthday would be the perfect time for such a celebration, and we co-ordinated our efforts with the cantor and learned the proper prayers and ceremonial readings. Determined not to slacken in our studies, we took our prayer books on the trip with us so that we could practice. God is in control, we told ourselves, and God will guide us toward fulfilling our plans.

On the all-important day of our trip to Las Vegas, we boarded the flight with renewed confidence and trust in God's wisdom. Slowly, we took our places in the three-seated aisle, with Esther sitting near the window, and I took the middle seat and an empty aisle seat beside me. Taking out our books, we began to recite our prayers in low voices not to disturb anyone on the plane.

Suddenly, an older man with a white beard approached and asked if we were praying in Hebrew.

I replied affirmatively.

"May I sit here?" the elder inquired, pointing to the empty seat.

"Of course," I said.

"Thank you. You know," the gentleman began. "I have traveled worldwide many times and never seen anyone praying in Hebrew during an entire flight. Are you praying because you are afraid or for some other reason?"

62
NOT EVERYTHING GOES RIGHT ALL THE TIME.
WHEN THINGS DO NOT TURN OUT ACCORDING TO OUR EXPECTATIONS,
WE HAVE COMPLETE FAITH THAT EVERYTHING WILL WORK FOR THE BEST

I smiled, "Neither of the above. My wife and I will celebrate our B'nai Mitzvah next month, and we are having a little diffi-culty with the Hebrew prayers. This is my wife, Esther."

The gentleman graciously shook hands with both of us.

"I speak Hebrew also, and I always say a short prayer – my personal favorite—which is very powerful and meaningful. If I may, I would like to recite it for you, as I believe it will assist you and your wife in all your endeavors," the gentleman offered.

I consented, and the gentleman proceeded:

"B'SHEM HASHEM NAAHASE V' NESLIACH."

"You said the prayer very quickly. Can you repeat it, please?"

I asked, impressed by the flow and beauty of the words. The gentleman repeated the phrase more slowly, enunciating each word. "When you say this prayer in faith, God will grant you the victories you seek. It means, "In the name of God, it will be done, and you will succeed."

I asked him, "Can you please write it in Hebrew and translate it for us?"

He agreed.

63
WHEN YOU LEAST EXPECT IT, GOD SENDS ANGELS TO PROVIDE YOU WITH A TESTIMONY OF FAITH

I was astounded. I began to think of all that Esther and I faced, including the B'nai Mitzvah ceremony and the apartment building loan, and suddenly felt that everything would turn out precisely as we believed it would.

"Please return to your seats and fasten your seatbelts as we descend into Las Vegas," the stewardess instructed the passen-gers over the loudspeaker.

64
**B' SHEM HASHEM NAASEH V' NATSLIACH—
"IN THE NAME OF GOD,
IT WILL BE DONE, AND
YOU WILL SUCCEED"**

I thanked the gentleman with all my heart and shook his hand. He then took his leave and returned to his seat.

"Can you believe what just happened here?" I turned to Esther in amazement. "By the grace of God, this gentleman was sent to reassure us that our B'nai Mitzvah and the apartment loan will turn out in our favor. I would like to take his name and contact information and thank him properly. Let's wait until everyone disembarks from the back of the plane, and when he passes by, we will stop him momentarily."

"That's a great idea. We'll just wait," Esther replied.

We waited ... and waited, looking carefully and scanning the faces of every passenger who passed by our seats, but no one even remotely resembled him.

"Hurry! Let's exit and try to catch up with him. Perhaps, we missed him in the crowd," I suggested.

We looked everywhere, but the gentleman was nowhere to be found, not even at the airport's luggage turnstile.

I turned to Esther and said, "This is a great gift God has given us. God sent an angel to meet us on the plane and let us know that our prayers will be answered through faith and we will attain victory. Also, he gave us the most incredible gift of the Hebrew prayer!" I exclaimed.

After we picked up our luggage, we searched for the nearest pay phone (at the time, we didn't have cell phones). "I'm going to call the banker, but before I do, let's say the Hebrew prayer that the angel gave us three times, affirming and believing that what we desire is already done and that God has granted us the victory," Esther said.

I pulled out the piece of paper where the angel had written the prayer and placed our faith in the outcome; we recited it three times, just as Esther suggested. We then called the banker.

"Marcos," he said in an upbeat tone. "I have excellent news for you. The loan was approved, and the closing will take place in three weeks."

Both of us couldn't believe our ears. In unison, we said, "Amen! Hallelujah! Glory to God and all the good angels." We then called our son Izzy and sister Rachel to tell them the news, and we all rejoiced.

65
WHEN WE LIVE BY FAITH, GOD PROVIDES US WITH THE VICTORY

It has been over twenty years since we met the angel, and since that time, we have continued to say the prayer that he taught us—the most beautiful we have ever heard. Each time we say that prayer, only the most favorable results come about, always to the glory of God. We have always believed in angels throughout our lives, but we never had such an astonishing confirmation of their existence as we experienced on the plane to Las Vegas in 1997.

Our Granddaughter's Encounter With An Angel

Not only do we have a story about an angel, but Sara, our dear granddaughter, also has experienced such visitations more than once. During a period of doubt and uncertainty in her life, Sara did her best to stay positive and go about her daily routine. One day, she drove to pick up her eyeglasses and parked across the street from her doctor's office. In the parking lot, an elderly gentleman holding a probiotic organic drink in his hand walked up and waved to her. "I'm intrigued by your black jeep, with its pink accents and USDA organic label on the side," he said.

"Thanks!" Sara exclaimed, opening the window slightly. "I'm advertising my website, which focuses on organic foods and lifestyles."

"That's great! I can't believe someone your age is raising people's awareness of the subject. Keep up the good work!" the man said encouragingly. "Well, I had better get going. My bike is parked just at the corner."

66
ANGELS NEED NOT HAVE
WINGS TO BE MESSENGERS
OF GOD. THEY CAN APPEAR
IN ALL SORTS OF WAYS AND
THE LEAST EXPECTED PLACES

Deeply moved by the inspiration the man had given her, Sara remained in her spot, turning her head to determine where he had gone. To her surprise, she could not see him anywhere. He seemed to have just vanished into thin air. Surveying the area more closely, she didn't see his bicycle or anyone resembling him. After a few moments of reflection, Sara concluded that she must have encountered an angel sent by God to uplift, inspire, and endorse her efforts at a time when she particularly needed that validation.

On another occasion, she was in the supermarket with her mother, Janice, retrieving a grocery cart when they saw a woman with a white aura surrounding her. A very distinct, positive energy seemed to emanate from her to both mother and daughter. Sara felt insecure about her physical appearance, although she is a very beautiful young woman (we are not biased grandparents. We only wish to express the truth). The woman paused beside them, turned to Sara, and said, "I just want to tell you that you are the most beautiful girl I have ever seen." Janice felt goose-bumps all over, and the biggest smile appeared on Sara's face. Once again, she had received a much-deserved confirmation of her worth—the inner and outer beauty evident to everyone who knows her. After speaking those words of positivity and light, the woman simply walked out of the store, into the darkness of night, without a trace. She was nowhere to be found, but her message lingered, and Sara's insecurities never resurfaced. She had received a message of light and hope that changed how she looked at herself and her place in the world.

In sharing our encounters with angels, we hope to give our readers a tool to pray in faith with affirmative results and believe that when good intentions are unleashed in the world, they will be validated. Such is our wish for you, our readers.

My Aunt Raquel always believed that "when you pray, you must display all our faith and unleash it. When you do, you will see that God takes pride in providing you with all you need. Sometimes, you will not receive everything you want, but God knows best, and you must trust God with everything. Also, listen to your subconscious mind and hear what God is telling you to do or say. Also, you must be alert to the signs God places in your surroundings and be aware of the negative brain chatter in your head or those that surround you through ill-willed people or those who don't believe."

The appearance of angels lets us know that none of us walks alone. God uses angels as affirmations for us. Anywhere and everywhere we go, God is present and willing to assist us in every circumstance. While we are in this world to complete our mission, our bodies naturally pull us down into the realm of materialism, and we are side-tracked from our true purpose. Fear, doubt, uncertainty, and a host of other feelings that come with being on Planet Earth are all manifestations of materialistic emotions and tendencies. Sometimes, however, when we least expect it, the presence of angels in our midst guides us on the path to self-fulfillment and light.

67
ANGELS CONFIRM GOD'S TRUTH THAT WE HARBOR INSIDE, BUT SOMETIMES IGNORE OR FAIL TO ACKNOWLEDGE

Even when we feel we walk in darkness, we must embrace the belief that angels exist to help us walk in faith and confi-dence. They are there for everyone—with faith, patience, and sincerity whenever we ask. Always remember that everything we go through is a test from

God. However, the Creator will send the appropriate angels to help lead us to victory. Angels are the torchbearers of peace, love, hope, and illumination on our journey.

> **68**
> **WE CAN ALL BE PART OF GOD'S ANGELIC ARMY BY HELPING OTHERS AND SPREADING WORDS AND ACTS OF LOVE AND KINDNESS**

How Do We Become Angels In This World?

God has sent us to this world to complete our mission and become Angels while we transition here on Earth. We are all called to be Angels of God and to be part of the Angelic Army. It is up to us to make that decision. Do we want to serve God? If so, people will tell us that we are like angels because we took that extra step to help someone, perform acts of love and kindness in our daily routine, or bring words of consolation and hope to others. We begin with our spouse, children, family, friends, or strangers, or when we demonstrate to others that we maintain our faith, no matter what may be happening in our lives, we show to the world that we are acting as angels because we put all our trust in God. We understand that everything happens for our good.

In evaluating our circumstances, we must ask ourselves whether we want to serve the material world and engage in acts of hate, anger, jealousy, selfishness, and other behaviors that tend to hurt and distress others, projecting unfaithfulness and destructive tendencies toward others and ourselves.

If we want to be part of the Angelic Army while we are in this world so that when we complete our mission, we can transition into eternal life as celestial beings, we need to arm ourselves with spiritual weapons every day before we move forward.

On page 115, you will find some affirmations with which to equip yourself with the necessary spiritual armor that will enable you to become part of God's Angelic Army

**69
SEEK AND ACT UPON
OPPORTUNITIES TO
BECOME GOD'S
SPIRITUAL AGENTS**

Lessons in Encountering Angels

Some people are skeptical about the existence of angels. Those who doubt feel more secure in believing in that which they can perceive, feel, and experience through the five senses. The certainty of the known universe makes them feel confident, alive, and grounded. Consider, however, the glory and beauty of existence beyond what we humans apprehend in our limited ways. So much "out there" exceeds the boundaries we place around ourselves to understand and know what exists, but what is "knowledge?" That is a significant question to ponder when considering the presence of angels in our midst. We propose that knowledge exists in two forms. The first is empirical knowledge – that level of understanding that is indisputable and can be proven and verified through firsthand experience or ob-servation. The second is subjective knowledge, which does not require proof, but is based solely on the viewer's perspective. Mathematical certainties belong in the first group, and opinions in the second. For example, the fact that 1+1 = 2 is indisput-able. However, if someone asks, "What is the most beautiful city in the world?" the answer is subjective, based on individual perspective.

Sometimes, the lines between empirical and subjective knowledge are blurred, and the two are not mutually exclusive. Angels hover in the in -betweens, showing us that everything is not merely black or white. God sends these messengers to heighten our awareness of what can be outside the narrow confines of our five senses—the filters we use to absorb and appreciate the world in which we live.

Some may ask, "Do angels—individuals whose capacities and wisdom far exceed ordinary humans—manifest in human form?" We answer affirmatively. According to our beliefs and convictions, based on our life experiences, we have confirmed that there are two types of angels. Some are spiritual beings (those that we do not see) . God uses those kinds of angels to protect, guide, educate, or help us in any situation where God desires to show a miracle to a particular person, family, or community. There are also those angels who are still in this world and whose primary purpose is to do the will and carry the message of God through acts of love, kindness, and blessings without looking for recognition or reward. They are content with the spiritual satisfaction derived from their God-given opportu-nity to be present at the very moment when they are needed in a given situation or speak through positive words of hope, love, and consolation. With the guidance of angels, people in need can turn their lives around, be open to receiving direction from God, and ultimately, be guided to victory.

We discovered this firsthand when our loan was denied. We knew that God had a greater plan for us, which could only mate-rialize if we let go and allowed Divine power to guide the course of our destiny. By embracing the angel's prayer, "B' SHEM HASHEM NAAHASE V' NESLIACH," we affirmed the ever-present guidance of Divine Will in our lives, and as a result, God granted us victory.

In like manner, the angels our granddaughter encountered gave her the universal, God-guided perspective that she needed—at just the right time—to validate her goals and give her the self-worth she had to cultivate to move forward in joy. When we understand that everything occurs according to Divine Purpose/ God-mind, we stop categorizing and labeling situations, people, and our lives. Invariably, labels give rise to negative conclu-sions. Good angels are extensions of God, beckoned by the Creator to carry out Divine Will and extend a helping hand in times of need. They exist to inspire and activate our higher con-sciousness so that we can appreciate that outcomes are ultimate-ly in God's hands.

A Personal Testimony About the Angel In China

A little background is required here to allow my readers to fully understand what happened to me recently while I was in China.

A day before we traveled to China in April 2018, our writing collaborator sent us the final manuscript for review before sending it to the press. I told her that Esther and I would have the opportunity to read it on the plane during the long flight. As it turned out, however, on the flight to China, we could proofread only three chapters.

The first day of our mission was in Beijing. The first two days after our arrival, the weather was very cold and rainy as we went through our mission. On the fourth day, I came down with a terrible cold. Thank God, we took some medicine from home, but after three days, I ran out of medicine. I decided to stay at the hotel to recuperate while everyone went on without me. Despite my ill feeling, I knew that God had a purpose— as in all things and that I would come to understand the situation in time. I told myself that perhaps, the objective was to continue to proofread the book alone and wait for Esther's input later that day.

At lunchtime, Esther called and asked me to go to the res-taurant and have some soup and ginger tea to help alleviate my cold. I did as Esther suggested and returned to our room to continue reading the manuscript. All the while, I felt feverish, and I had the chills. Feeling sick and sleepy, I lay down in bed to take a nap after I thoroughly read this very Chapter 6. I wanted to call my wife but did not want to worry her, as there was little that she could do at a distance of one and a half hours.

I awakened an hour later, feeling very stuffy and coughing. It was about three o'clock when I heard the doorbell ringing. As I went to open the door, I saw the mission coordinator, with his hand outstretched, offering me Chinese medicine for my cold. He said, "I stayed here because I had to run some errands, and Esther called to request that I bring some medicine to help you, and here I am." He proceeded to instruct me as to how I should take the medication called "Sunshine."

"Can I begin now?" I asked.

"Of course. Take the medication now and later at night. Then, before you go to bed, you take the special herbs you make (like tea)," he replied.

Immediately after I took the medication, I felt some relief. "You have been the angel that God sent me to help with my cold," I said gratefully.

"No." He smiled. "Esther was the one who called me."

"In that case, Esther served as the angel who received the message from God and acted upon it to call you, and, in turn, you were the angel who responded to the call to bring the cold medicine."

"OK. Whatever you believe. You know that I do not believe in God or angels, but I was glad to help," the man replied, looking at me earnestly.

"How much do I owe you for the medicine?" I inquired.

"Nothing. That is on me," he said as he departed.

This story demonstrates how God uses everyone—even those who do not believe in a Supreme Being or angels —to act as angels in this world.

Angelic Energy is universal and part of God's Grand Design, pervading the heavens and earth. Look for the signs.

In pledging to become part of God's Angelic Army, I humbly ask the Creator to grant me the opportunity to be a positive influence in the lives of others, spreading kindness wherever I go and in all instances, even when I am challenged. May all my worries and doubts disappear because FEAR = FALSE EVIDENCE APPEARING REAL

True Faith in God Casts Off Uncertainty and Doubt

CHAPTER 7

THE REASONS WE SHOULD NOT ASK GOD "WHY?"

God has given each person free will, which also involves the freedom to question divine intention and everything that happens in their lives.

With our limited human understanding, we always question circumstances we do not understand. God wants to assist us in growing our faith. This is why our Creator provides us with the knowledge, little by little, as we grow older —and, most signifi-cantly, as our faith increases. Those incomprehensible events sometimes leave us confused, depressed, and seeking answers. The questions may be challenging, but the answers are simple for those who have chosen to take a leap of faith and believe that God is the supreme, omniscient, benevolent, spiritual, super-natural, eternal energy force—the Creator of the universe and all that exists. God is the infinite Source of positive energy and knows what was, what is, and what will be. Those who have decided to live by faith in God find all their answers in the very existence of God. The fact that God IS serves as the complete answer, above and beyond the physical world, where questions are limited to our five senses - Those who are skeptical and do not want to believe in anything that they cannot filter through their five senses are determined to believe only in things of the physical world—to the negation of the spiritual. These indi-viduals find it challenging to understand the ways of God. No matter what anyone may tell them, the explanations will be apprehended through their own values and belief systems, and they will remain unconvinced, living with their own ways until the right time when God determines that the veil will be lifted from their eyes. This leads to the perpetual question asked by those constantly seeking to know the "Why?" of everything.

70
QUESTIONING WHY IS THE BIGGEST FORM OF REBELLION, AND BLOCKS OUT FAITH IN GOD

Asking God, "Why?" is the most blatant form of rebellion and eliminates all possibilities of having faith in God. We have the free will to do whatever we want and ask about what we do not understand. We can use excuses for not receiving the answer that satisfies us or conforms to the answer we seek or desire. In such cases, we can say that this is why we do not believe in the existence of God. The question then becomes, "If God truly existed, why do negative things occur in our lives and the world at large? The error of this question lies in the fact that in asking "why," we are not looking to God for peace, knowledge, or un-derstanding through faith. We are just expressing our rebellion and telling God that we do not accept one situation or another. We just tend to seek satisfactory answers, and when we do not feel fulfilled in our request, we ask, "How can we believe in God when the answer is unclear to us?"

Questioning the creation of the universe, our mission and purpose as human beings, and eternal life paves the way for us to doubt and cling to uncertainty that leads us on a path of spiritual crisis. Asking "why?" prompts our souls not to believe in God and to live a life of rebellion against our Creator. As a result, we live daily in doubt, fear, mental wrangling, and un-happiness, and we cannot find positive answers to our questions. Individuals who think in such a way always question, "WHY is this happening to me?" Most of the time, they will sabotage any prosperity that comes their way or decision-making in their personal or professional lives, whether the decision pertains to health, relationships, or other concerns.

For those souls who have found and nurtured their faith, the questions are unnecessary because their faith does not waver. Instead of doubting and seeking, people of faith raise their eyes and say, "God, please, show me the way and the purpose for all of the trials and tribulations I am experiencing. Help me to see that your reasoning and planning will lead me on a better path in life. Although I don't understand your reasons now, I trust you and know that everything will turn out for the best. I believe you will provide me with the proper solutions at the appropriate time. I love you and trust in your decisions.

I thank you for giving me the understanding that everything will happen on your timetable, not mine. Help me to maintain my faith and patience to weather the storms." This simple dec-laration will provide you with the peace you require, and God will be delighted to deliver the answers and reasons that we seek later, sometimes sooner than we expect. Sometimes God's answer may take one hour, day, week, or longer than we could ever expect. The length and profundity of the question and the solution to our challenges depend on our degree of faith. Even if it takes longer than we may expect for answers to be revealed to us, God wants to ensure that we don't continue to question divine timing. Some prayers take longer to manifest than others, but in the end, everything works out according to God's plan.

Today, we must ask God to give us more opportunities to demonstrate love and kindness and perform charitable acts to elevate our souls and get closer to the Divine. When this occurs, we never ask God "why" because we understand that if God wants us to endure pain, suffering, or losses, we can correct our mistakes and transform them into testimonies of faith. In so doing, we depurate our souls and reap the fruits of satisfaction and reward in this world and the next.

Therefore, instead of questioning, "why?" we will realize that our trials are only temporary, and we will say, "Please, God, help us to overcome our trials so that we can use them as foundational lessons for confronting future tests and sharing them as testimonies of faith with others."

71
DOUBT AND FEAR LEAD TO PERPETUAL STRUGGLE AND CONFUSION. DWELLING IN FAITH IN GOD YIELDS ACCEPTANCE AND A CLEAR VISION

Are You Mentally Wavering Between Doubt and Faith?

Many people have struggled with the question, "Should I have faith or give in to doubts?" to this day, many souls among us now constantly wrestle with God and are always asking, "Why is this happening to me?"

Each one of the decisions that we make will bring us to a destination that will show us whether we have made the right choices or not. God created the laws of cause and effect for many reasons. How we choose to think and act directly impacts the outcome of our decisions, and we have free will to decide for ourselves. God will not force us to love, obey and follow Divine instructions. God loves us no matter what occurs and how long it will take to love the Creator in return and follow the Divine will. Unconditionally, God will be there for us to receive Divine love. Even after we make the worst mistakes and end up in the most unfavorable circumstances, God will still grant us opportunities for new beginnings—if we only request God's guidance, forgiveness, and love.

Based on our experiences with success and failure during our lives, we have found that once we accept God's divinity and invite the Creator into our lives, things begin to change for the better. Those who have faith in God are granted the knowledge and spiritual armor to overcome all the challenges and tests the Creator puts before us. As a result, these believers confront every test with peace and the knowledge that they will be victo-rious and receive abundant love, good health, success, wealth, happiness, and peace in every sphere of life—business, professional, and personal relationships. In other words, when all of us invite the most powerful, knowledgeable Coach into our lives, we will be equipped with the spiritual weapons that strength-en and make us greater than our challenges. As a result, we can accomplish our goals and go from victory to victory. This does not mean the believer in God does not have to go through pain, sickness, failure, distress, and disaster. In all situations, remember that God has a reason and a purpose for everything to happen as it does.

72
**EVERY CHALLENGE IS A LESSON
FOR FUTURE TESTS THAT WILL BECOME
TESTIMONIES OF FAITH THROUGH BELIEF IN GOD**

Mourning Our Relatives When They Pass On is a Gift From God

When mourning our relatives who pass on to the next world, we usually have many questions for God and "whys." We believe that when they left the earth and their physical bodies were buried, God granted them a new spiritual body. Depending on how they lived and conducted themselves in the physical world, God will direct the course of their eternal lives and instruct the angel to guide that spirit to the proper place of rest or a waiting station.

While in mourning, we can help the spirits of our relatives in the spiritual world by praying for them, trusting that God will consider all their good deeds and intentions, also remem-bering the legacies that they left us, performing acts of love and kindness on their behalf, and speaking with joy about the contributions that they made to us and others in the physical world. These gestures will be our deposits before God as we seek divine mercy for our families' souls in the world to come.

73
GRIEVING FOR THE DEPARTURE OF OUR LOVED ONE, IS ALSO AN OPPORTUNITY TO REFLECT ON THEIR CONTRIBUTIONS TO THE WORLD

In our personal experience, when our loved ones transitioned into the next world, we were not sad because we knew they had fulfilled their mission and performed many acts of love and kindness. At the same time, we were aware that we did everything in our power to make them comfortable; we loved and respected them and did everything we could to help them while they were here and in their last days. Therefore, we were satisfied and thanked God for granting us the opportunity to be there for them as they were for us throughout their lives.

When God takes our loved ones, we assume they have completed their mission in this world and will be granted their earned place of eternal peace and rest. We must complete the blessing of mourning for our loved ones because by doing so, we realize that God listens to our prayers, our loved one's spirits hear what we are saying about the memories and legacies that they left us, and they rejoice to hear about them. We also have an opportunity to meditate and draw conclusions about what we must do to prepare for our eventual departure from Planet Earth.

In times of mourning, we all must appreciate our family and friends who come to our side to console us and provide words of wisdom and strength to continue our life's journey. That act is a gift to those who have left the physical world.

Should We Question God's Reasons For Taking Those Whom We Love and Care About Before Their Time?

**74
EVERYONE HAS A TIME
AND A PURPOSE TO COMPLETE
THEIR MISSION ACCORDING
TO GOD'S WILL**

When we accept God's will, we understand that no matter what happens in our lives, all is for the best, and at the same time, when we understand that our purpose in life is to elevate our souls, we will understand that each person must fulfill their mission according to God's will. For all of us, that mission is to perform acts of love and kindness, accept and treat everyone as equals, correct our wrongdoings, help others as much as we can, pray daily, and live each day as if tomorrow were our last day on earth. When the time comes for God to call us to leave this world, we will be ready to accept our spiritual bodies, and God will take us to our place of rest and peace. Therefore, we need not question God's will when our loved ones pass away at an early or older age or when we end our own lives. We must accept that

God, the Creator of the universe, knows how much time we must live here on earth, and therefore, in whatever we do, we must do our best. Who are we to ask God why some people must depart earlier than others? Sometimes a newborn baby lives for only days. As difficult to understand as it may seem, God had a reason for granting that baby such a brief time on earth. Maybe, the baby's spirit had to come to this world at a certain time, or perhaps; God was testing the parents' willing-ness to turn their lives around, have more trust in the Divine, and make a greater deposit in their spiritual bank account, instead of turning the incident into something negative and de-stroying their marriage, as a result. If the couple trusts in God and moves on with their lives through their mourning period, the Creator will provide them with other children, who must be received with love, and God will grant them the opportunity to use the tragedy to benefit others and themselves. They should not be sad that the other baby did not make it. Instead, they should thank God and dedicate themselves to helping their new children become individuals of purpose and goodwill. By doing so, they will pass their test, and when the time comes, they will be able to reunite with their lost child in eternity.

Sometimes, parents lose children not only in infancy but also after they graduate from high school or college. Young people may be subjected to challenges and dire circumstances that may even cause them to face death (either through accident or disease). We are devastated and angry in our grief and condemn God for allowing such things to happen. But God does not provide us with a guarantee of how many years we are going to be in this world or how long our relatives are going to live. This is why the only thing we have today is to do our best to express our love and action of kindness to our loved ones and those that surround us.

75
WE CALL TODAY "THE PRESENT" BECAUSE IT IS THE GIFT THAT GOD GIVES US EACH DAY

As difficult as it may be, we must give ourselves time to mourn and thank God for the years these individuals were given on earth with those they loved and those who loved them. We must remember the legacies they left behind—even though they were so young—and promote good works in their memories through acts of charity and fundraising for a specific cause in their names, perpetuating their legacies in every way possible. Then, all we can do is move forward and incorporate their memories into our lives while purifying our souls by performing acts of love and kindness. Blaming, judging, or questioning God should not occupy our attention. Instead, we must concentrate on correcting our mistakes and using the abundance that God has provided us to help others.

Why Do We Mentally Wrestle with Ourselves When Making Decisions?

As human beings, our job is to create a balance between the earthly and spiritual energies that are constantly pulling us in different directions. God created our spirits to incarnate into the body so that the spirit can correct its wrongdoing from a previous life and ascend into the realm of eternal life. At the same time, the spirit understands that the body has needs and desires, and by helping the body to achieve its objectives, the spirit grows, as well. On the other hand, if the body takes control of the de-cision-making process and does not accept that the incarnated spirit must complete its mission, the flesh will reject God's will, and the body may experience adverse effects in the physical world and avoid spiritual growth in the eternal sphere. For this reason, we are constantly wrestling with conflicts between the body and the spirit, and therefore, decision-making becomes very difficult.

76
SINCE THE BEGINNING OF THE WORLD,
GOD HAS MADE KNOWN TO
HUMANKIND THE COMMANDS
THAT WE MUST FOLLOW ON EARTH
TO LIVE PEACEFULLY AND RECEIVE ETERNAL LIFE

Has God Provided Us with Instructions on How to Live?

God has instructed many messengers in various countries to write and provide us with the message our Creator wants us to follow. Each religion may present the message in different ways and languages, but when you read each scroll, you will find that they all have the same intent and meaning:

To love one another, treat your fellow human being as you wish to be treated, be kind and just to everyone, and ask for for-giveness if you offend your neighbor or a family member. In the end, it all comes down to the same basic principle. Even today, in many different parts of the world, there are people continu-ously delivering the message of faith, love, peace, and eternal life—instructions to guide us in living an abundant life in this world and attaining eternal life.

> **77**
> WE CANNOT EXPECT TO UNDERSTAND GOD'S PLAN ENTIRELY UNTIL OUR MISSION IS COMPLETED. THEREFORE, TRUST IN THE CREATOR, BE THANKFUL, AND DO WHAT IS BEST IN THE EYES OF GOD

When Destruction and Suffering Occur, How Should People React?

Let's agree to embrace the idea that earthly life is not eternal and that eternity is granted to the spirit only when it fulfills its mission in the physical world. By accepting that concept, we can withstand our trials and move forward. Our spirits con-stantly evolve until their respective missions on earth have been fulfilled. Everything that occurs is designed to help us manifest and complete those missions. When we apply faith to whatever we must face by believing that our challenges exist for our benefit while we are on earth, those rewards continue into eternity. We must accept and embrace God's purpose. God may provide us the opportunity to discover the reason and purpose for the tests that we are going through, either immediately or at a later time. Either by way of a person, a book, a television program, or the little voice inside us, we will encounter the answers we seek. If God calls upon us and our bodies die, our spirits are lifted into eternity and will face our Creator. At that time, we will be able to see all the tests we went through, the victories and failures we experienced on earth, and the purpose of the various difficulties we faced. We also will understand what God wanted us to ac-complish in the world.

Even amid destruction and suffering, God is showing Divine goodness. God presents us with different tests and tribulations because the Creator intends for goodness to follow destruction by allowing us to regroup in our spiritual and family circles, either through personal or collective challenges. God wants us to be kinder, humbler, more charitable, to love one another or simply to be more trusting in the Divine Source. It is better to correct our wrongdoings while we are alive on this planet than to come before God, having forfeited the opportunity to do good work in this life.

Each day, when we wake up, God presents us with one more opportunity to live our lives according to the Grand Scheme, correct our past mistakes, and ask our Creator to allow us to spread acts of love and goodwill to our fellow human beings. In this way, we elevate our spirits and move closer to the Divine.

78
WE ARE SOULS INCARNATED WITH VARIOUS MISSIONS AND LESSONS TO LEARN ALONG THE WAY

When we walk in faith with God, we gain understanding and wisdom through various tests. Sometimes God gives us another means of attaining the health we require, success and abundance. Therefore, to label people or circumstances "good" or "bad" is not according to God's intention. Everything that happens in our lives is for our own good.

Each of us has a different mission and tests—no matter where we are born and regardless of our racial, cultural, or edu-cational backgrounds. Outward appearance is just a visual dif-ferentiation God uses to determine whether we treat one another with respect and equality or intentionally feel superior based on superficial criteria, such as socioeconomic status and physical, cultural, or religious differences. We all have the same purpose—even if we have various hues of skin colors, speak different languages, or worship God in different ways. We are all here to help one another to fulfill our purposes and to show that the love we share is the love that God wants us to spread on earth. Most of the time, the goodness that God wants us to practice derives from hardship. We must love everyone as equals, but we do not have to accept those who commit acts of violence or cause pain or harm to other human beings.

**79
THE LOVE THAT WE SHARE
IS A GIFT THAT GOD WANTS
US TO SPREAD TO EVERYONE IN THE WORLD**

Some believe that when we are born, the Angel of Life touches us on the upper lips, and we, as babies, then forget our previous lives. In this way, God designs the evolution of spirits; but God does not want us to have memories of the previous life or a vision of the past or future. The mysteries of the soul's spiritual evolution on earth and in eternity are very profound and require intense study to understand the subject. Of course, we will not be able to know all the secrets of God and the mysticism of the spirit world until we complete our missions, at which time, our spirits will achieve the required level of understanding. Therefore, we must strive to perform acts of love and kindness, repent when we sin, become part of God's Angelic Army, and be willing to bless everyone in God's name.

Understanding Our Purpose

Instead of becoming caught up in the "whys" of life, we must dedicate ourselves to fulfilling the mission for which we were sent to

SUCCESS & PROSPERITY

earth. Questioning and doubt are unproductive because they take us away from the ultimate purpose of our mission: to glorify God and to commit ourselves to acts of loving kindness on earth.

When we doubt, we often become confused, depressed, and directionless; but when we focus in prayer on what truly matters, we will be able to shoulder and understand the often incompre-hensible events that take place during our lifetimes.

Through good and tough times, we must realize that God has a purpose for everything and that Divine Will surpasses limited human comprehension. If we let go of our overpower- ing, limited resources and let God direct our steps, we will experi-ence a shower of blessings:

80
FOCUS ON THE MISSION, NOT THE "WHYS" AND THE STRUGGLES. IN SO DOING, MAINTAINING FAITH IN GOD MUST BE SUPREME

Storms will turn into calmness.
Sickness will transform into health.
Lack will become abundance.
Loneliness will lead us to the right companion.
Seemingly unresolvable problems will be stepping stones to victory.
Darkness will fade into the light of day.

81
**WHEN YOU CONVERT YOUR
"WHYS" INTO TRUSTING GOD
THROUGH FAITH, YOUR LIFE CHANGES
AND GOD GRANTS YOU VICTORIES**

God works in Divine Time to assist human beings in their desired dreams and objectives. Our purpose, therefore, is to be devotional, steadfast, and true to God while resisting the human tendency to waver, fear, and doubt. Our mission will become clear, and we can proceed toward our true purpose.

Everything in our universe operates in complete balance—a perfect equilibrium of opposites: the forces of gravity, winter-summer, darkness-light, prosperity-impoverishment, good-evil, health-sickness, love-hate, and countless other contrast-ing elements. These are examples of how God, with infinite wisdom, created the world. God does not want to force us to recognize the majesty and power with which Source- energy controls everything. Instead, God gave us free will to love and accept divinity or deny and reject Divine intervention in our lives.

We must follow God's example to structure our lives, em-phasizing needs and wants equally, between family time and work time and between worshiping God and focusing on other thoughts. My mother always told me that I understood the concept of balance in life and practiced it in my daily routine and relationships. I maintain a balanced life with my wife and family to the best of my ability. Our mission in life is to perform acts of love and kindness, give to charities, and believe that God is at work for our ultimate benefit. When acting according to these principles, we demonstrate that we are part of God's creation, and regardless of what happens in life, God's love dwells within us.

**82
PRAY TO STAY IN FAITH.
GOD WILL GUIDE YOUR STEPS, AND YOU WILL NOT
HAVE ANY MORE FEAR OR DOUBT**

Lessons in Recognizing the Presence of God

Most likely, all of us would agree that we did not arrive on this planet by accident. Something had to happen to breathe life into every living entity. That "something"—or someone - is God, the Creative Designer and Ultimate Life Artist. When we recognize that God is the Supreme Architect of our lives, we come to appreciate what this world has to offer, its awe -inspir-ing beauty, joys, sorrows, and yes, even its tribulations; for ev-erything is the handiwork of a Mind far greater than ours and ultimately beyond our understanding.

Yet, God is not inaccessible. On the contrary, the Creator dwells in every one of us. The glory that we perceive outside of us also resides within us. Everything on the planet is intercon-nected by a Prime Mover or Source that guides the way with light and wisdom, and if we only listen to the little whispers inside of us, we will find reasons to believe in God's existence.

There is nothing mysterious about God because the Almighty is as close as our heartbeats and in each breath we take. God is as real as the birds that fly and the plants that live around us. We need not fear or worry about things of this world that sometimes cause us daily strife because it is all part of an Infinitely Grand Design that only God understands. When we recognize the in-dwelling God (the presence of God within us), we doubt no more because we can hear the wisdom of the ages, the Truth that guides our journey, and with this understanding, we can continue to fulfill our mission in peace and without fear, because God will be with us all the days of our lives.

Prayer For Turning Whys Into Faith

Dear God,

Help me to see that everything that surrounds me is part of your Creation.
Provide me with wisdom to see that everything that occurs is for my good.
Help me to get up each morning with an attitude of gratitude.
Assist me in closing my mouth when I am tempted to confront you by asking "why?"

When things do not go as I anticipate, give me the patience to wait for things to happen in your time. I thank you, God, for helping me to convert my "whys" into faith and trust in you.

Amen.

**Do not question 'why.'
Instead, surrender the answer to God**

CHAPTER 8

TESTS OF OUR FAITH

Through our ups and downs, challenges, and tribulations, we are convinced that God is always in control and testing our faith. God always presents different tests in our path to give us the opportunity for us to grow in our faith and determine how we react and what we do under specific circumstances. These tests help us develop in mind, body, and spirit. Once we pass the tests and receive victory, we can use our experiences as testimonies for future tests and help others around us to see how great God is when we believe that the Master of the Universe is in control.

Whatever happens, and no matter what obstacles obstruct our way, we should always maintain faith, believing that God is present in our midst and that everything that is happening is for our best, for each of God's tests always has a purpose for our benefit. God will not allow anything to happen in our lives that is not for our benefit and spiritual growth. We only see with earthly eyes, but God knows and understands the bigger picture.

If we allow ourselves to see through the eyes of God with our faith, we will see with our spiritual eyes and be secure and comforted by the fact that everything is under control. When we believe, we attract that which we desire into our lives, but when we doubt, we also call forth what we envision, and we will witness the outcome. However, if we think negative-ly, our thoughts will generate more doubts, fear, uncertainty, and illness, and the outcomes will be worse than we imagined because they are not in God's program. We often act as though we want to handle things alone and do not allow God to help us and be involved in our lives.

83
EMBRACE AND ACKNOWLEDGE GOD'S SHIELD OF PROTECTION AROUND YOU

God is waiting to send us all the good angels to work for our benefit. Just turn to faith and stay there, and you will see good things happen, such as prosperity, healing, love, and peace that pours forth to you and your family. Allow the shield of pro-tection to encircle you and stay inside the Circle of Love God provided for you. Only we can break that protective shield by allowing fear, doubt, animosity, arguments, negative thoughts, and actions to enter our minds.

How Tests of Faith Have Led Us to the Blessings of Success and Spiritual Growth

I was sixteen years old and a new immigrant to the United States when I began to work in a factory that manufactured Christmas lights. The factory was in Brooklyn, New York, owned by my paternal cousins. They were very kind and allowed me to earn money. After I finished work and on my days off, I visited my Aunt Raquel and Uncle Angel.

TESTS OF OUR FAITH

After Every Storm, God Sends a Rainbow. Keep Looking Up!

I loved to listen to the stories that Uncle Angel would tell me about his experiences during his early years when he lived in New York. Tía Raquel would always look for every opportunity to teach me about spirituality, faith and belief in God, love, per-sistence, obedience, and engaging in acts of love, kindness, and repentance. She also emphasized that God is always in control and the Ultimate Provider, endowed with the knowledge that we have a soul (spirit) and a body. Since I was a child, Aunt Raquel taught me that although this life is temporary, the spirit lives forever. She would go deeply into many fascinating spiritual subjects.

84
RECOGNIZE THE SPIRIT OF DISCERNMENT AND PUT ITS POWER INTO PRACTICE

TESTS OF OUR FAITH

I absorbed her teachings and the simple examples she gave me about how to succeed while I strove to attain eternal peace in the world and complete my mission. She always told me never to be afraid of anything or anyone—no matter the circumstance. As long as I believed that God and the good angels protected me and I maintained my faith, nothing would happen to me. She emphasized that God would provide many different tests to help me grow in faith and assure me that the Divine Source would never abandon me under any circumstances.

I asked Tía Raquel, "What does having the spirit of discern-ment mean?" She said, "The spirit of discernment is represented by the special angel that God sends us so that we can understand our thoughts and intentions and those of others we encounter. That is one of the most significant weapons we require in our spiritual arsenal because many deceptive people and thoughts masquerade as good, but their intention is to cause harm."

Sooner than expected, I came to understand the importance of that lesson. I left work on one beautiful summer day and visited Tía Raquel and Uncle Angel. I took the train and disem-barked three stations past my destination. As I stepped off the subway and exited the station, three young men approached and cornered me against the building adjacent to the station. One displayed a gun and demanded that I give them the money or they would take it anyway and injure me. Recalling my Aunt Raquel's teachings, I told myself this was only a test, and God would not abandon or forsake me. I began to pray silently, asking God for guidance and assistance, and I requested the presence of the spirit of discernment. The young men were very impatient and continued to taunt me with threats. I realized that the gang also spoke Spanish. Suddenly, I felt like an army of angelic beings was in my midst.

Mustering my courage, I said to them in Spanish, "I am a new immigrant in this country, and I have very little money, but if you want me to share some of my money, I will share it with you in the name of God. I only have five dollars in my pocket."

One of the gang members grabbed me and tried to force his hand into my pocket, but I stepped back and said, "Wait one minute. Do you think I should be afraid of you because you have a gun in your hand that can kill me? If God wants me to go to eternal life, God knows I am prepared, but what about you guys? Are you prepared to meet your maker and respond to God with what you have been doing?"

The gang members froze, and one said, "Come on! This guy is a religious freak, and I don't need to listen to his sermon. Let him go, and let's move on to our next victim.

**85
DO NOT FEAR THE FORCES
OF EVIL. HAVE FAITH AND
GOD'S ANGELIC ARMY IS ALWAYS
READY TO HELP YOU**

As the three walked away, I pulled out my five dollars in singles and called out, "Here is one dollar for each of you to take as a seed of faith. God wants you to embrace them, with the expectation that you will change your lives, and God will show all of you how our Creator can provide you with abundance without your having to mug people."

The three gang members took the three dollars, and one of them said, "Come, let's accompany him to make sure that nothing happens to him."

When I reached my aunt's house and told them what happened, Aunt Raquel raised her hand and thanked God for testing me and allowing me to emerge victoriously. I replied, "I cannot understand why God allows bad people to exist."

86
GOD ACTS AS OUR INSTRUCTOR IN THE CLASSROOM OF LIFE

"Come and sit down, and I will explain," Aunt Raquel replied. Pausing momentarily to reflect, she continued, "Each of us has a mission in this life and a purpose to fulfill that mission. Those spirits that allow their bodies to run the race to gain personal satisfaction by harming or taking advantage of others reject God's will and do not believe in God's existence or fear eternal life. However, God uses them like an arrow in an archer's hand to test those who are determined to follow God."

Aunt Raquel paused again and asked, "When you go to school, do the teachers test you to see if you have learned your lessons?"

"Yes," I said, nodding.

"Well, without these tests, the instructor would never know the degree to which you have learned and absorbed the material shown to you. God uses the same technique to gauge where we are on our path in life, our faith, acts of love and kindness, sincerity to repent for our mistakes, and our capacity to identify those we have accumulated from a previous lifetime. You have passed this test today because you did not fear anything. Instead, you trusted that the presence of God was with you, and God sent angels to strengthen, protect and guide you, but you have to remember that lesson well in the future. Sometimes, when we make mistakes, doubt, or fear, we show our faith is weak. So, God gives us different kinds of tests. At times, these tests have to do with our own or our family's health, a loved one's departure, the loss of a job or material possessions, or other challenges that force us to reflect on our life or our lack of faith. "By teaching and testing us, God acts like a parent, teacher, or coach, allowing us to understand where we went wrong, correct our mistakes, and return to our mission. Usually, parents just tell their children when they have done something wrong, and the children learn their lesson; but at other times, parents instruct their children to ponder the error of their ways to conclude that they have gone astray. God uses these same techniques to guide us on the path of righteousness. When we are tested, our only recourse is to ask God for forgiveness with a sincere heart and promise that we will not transgress again, and when we are con-fronted with further tests, we will act appropriately.

**87
GOD ACTS LIKE A PARENT,
TEACHER OR COACH, WHO
ALLOWS US TO UNDERSTAND
THE LESSONS IN OUR TESTS**

The Lessons In Our Tests

"You must understand that most people resent God for the terrible things that happen to them. That is the reason why some people remain apart from God. Remember that God is a God of mercy, love, and compassion that we must emulate."

I soon realized that my experience in the subway station served as a test that I ultimately converted into a testimony. The lessons I learned helped me grow in faith, conquer my fears and go from victory to victory. When I thanked Aunt Raquel for such a life-changing lesson, she replied, "The one whom you must thank is God, who loves you so much and wants to teach you this lesson of faith and courage at an early age."

Many years later, I had to confront a similar test. Because the lessons derived from the experience with the three gang members were deeply embedded in my mind and heart, I imme-diately relived that day. I was able to overcome whatever I had to face with more confidence.

That lesson has remained with me throughout many different challenges, and I am proud to say that God has helped me emerge victoriously in each instance. The Divine Source has guided me to this moment to share and summarize my thoughts with you and to inspire you to walk with God in faith. If you do so, you will witness many victories in your life.

**88
WALK IN FAITH, AND
YOU WILL ULTIMATELY
WALK INTO VICTORY**

Lessons In Endurance

In this life, we are constantly tested to determine how we react to different situations. Whatever obstacles are in our way, we should always believe God is in control. God will not allow anything to happen in our lives that will not enable us to use our God-given power to see with the eyes of faith. We must witness all of the good things God has prepared for us as we move forward in our lives.

If you read this affirmation and the Prayer of Faith (above) every day, absorb and practice them, you will witness the differ-ence in your life and the prosperity, peace, health, and happiness God will bring you by believing.

Prayer of Faith

Dear God,

Allow me to perceive each of life's tests through the eyes of faith, not with my physical sight.

Do not allow the night's darkness to envelop my soul. Instead, give me the strength to confront all my trials with faith, like the sun you bestow upon Planet Earth each morning that illuminates my path to victory.

I trust that your will be done.

Amen.

Nothing Grows Without Struggle

CHAPTER 9

FROM A CELEBRATION TO A TEST, FROM TRIBULATION TO VICTORY

**89
PRAY TO GOD FOR GUIDANCE
AND GOD WILL HELP YOU TO
TRANSFORM YOUR LIFE**

In our own lives, we have not been strangers to God's tests of our faith. The following story illustrates this point. It was the summer of 2012, and our nephew, Leon, was planning to get married in Paris, France. There were a lot of expectations leading up to the wedding, along with the hustle-bustle and commotion that preceded that event. Intent on making their wedding unforgettable, the couple

SUCCESS & PROSPERITY

decided to marry in a castle. Our entire close family was excited to attend the spectacular wedding and take in the sights of Paris.

A couple of days before the big event, the family flew to Paris. Our son, Izzy, and his daughters, Sara and Mindy, flew to England, stopped to sightsee in London, then took the train to Paris to meet with the rest of the family. We toured various places, including an organic market, which was particularly in-teresting to our granddaughter, Sara. After dinner, Izzy called to suggest that we take a boat tour around the Eiffel Tower. Rachel and Esther were eager to go, but Sal (my brother-in-law) and I felt tired and tried to convince the ladies to reconsider; they ulti-mately felt compelled to see the Eiffel Tower at night since they would only stay a couple of days after the wedding. Rachel's older son, Benny, his wife, Galina, the children, and Esther left for the boat tour that would take them around the Eiffel Tower. They were having a wonderful time, and Esther was busy taking pictures to capture the memories, as she always loved to do. Around 11:00 p.m., I received her call stating that she had fallen on the boat.

90
NEVER ALLOW YOUR FAITH
TO WAVER IN MOMENTS OF
CRISIS. THAT IS THE TIME
WHEN YOU NEED IT THE MOST

"How seriously are you injured?" I asked with deep concern.

"I'm not sure. All I know is that I am in terrible pain and cannot move my arm," my wife replied.

Immediately, Rachel called Leon to accompany his father-in-law, a renowned doctor in France, who arrived in about fifteen minutes. After checking Esther's arm, the doctor decided that she should go to the hospital. First, however, they came to pick me up at the hotel. Although deeply concerned, I started praying and trusting that God had a purpose and a reason for everything, and I had faith that we would see the way.

When we arrived at the emergency room, it was packed with many injured people. Thank God Leon's father-in- law was very well known at the hospital and was able to bring Esther in for X-rays. Because of the late hour, the orthopedist was awakened and came to the hospital three hours later to read the X -Rays and diagnose: Esther's shoulder cup had been fractured in many different places. The discomfort was enormous, and the doctor informed her that she would require an entire shoulder cup re-placement. Of course, Esther's great preoccupation, along with her ailment, was attending Leon's wedding that afternoon. She did not want to miss that event under any circumstances.

"How long can I wait before I decide on the surgery?" she asked her doctor.

"About a week to ten days, but given the severity of the fractures, I would advise you not to wait," the doctor said solemnly.

I prayed to God and all the good angels for protection and guidance, and so did Esther as she quietly and patiently bore her suffering. After considering the matter, she declared, "I've decided that I will just have my shoulder wrapped, and I will attend the wedding as planned. We will cut our trip short and leave right after the wedding if we can book a seat on an immediate flight out. I will go ahead with the surgery in the U.S. under the guidance of my own physicians."

The doctor agreed. Leon and his father-in-law took us back to the hotel and then left to prepare for the big event. I then called the airline, and by the grace of God, a flight was available at the desired time. I was shocked that Esther was so calm and her pain had subsided. We slept for a few hours, had brunch, and then rested for a while before getting dressed and preparing to take the bus to the castle.

91
BEAR SUFFERING WITH PATIENCE, KNOWING THAT THE OUTCOME IS IN GOD'S HANDS – WITH A PURPOSE

Esther was a pillar of strength at the wedding and acted as though nothing had happened. Her courage in the face of adversity was remarkable—and she didn't take any of the pain medications prescribed at the hospital. She danced, mingled, and took photographs with ease, all the while praising God for the good fortune of being able to attend the wedding. "Everything is a test in life, and even though God allowed this to happen, there is a divine purpose for everything," I said.

When we arrived back in the States, Galina called the orthopedic doctor she knew, who agreed to see my wife the next day. He took X-rays and confirmed that she required a complete shoulder replacement. The surgery was scheduled for two days later. In the meantime, Esther and I returned to the apartment and tried to rest and sleep. We prayed and glorified God, knowing that our Creator would assist us in communicating with the doctors, nurses, and their staff regarding the surgery. "Don't worry, Mi Amor," I said. "I will go with you to the hospital and leave when you are discharged."

I kept that promise to Esther and was so overwhelmed that God provided us a suite with a bench and comfortable cushions that converted into a bed where I could sleep. The doctor agreed to my presence there at all times. On the night before the procedure, we prayed together, giving thanks for God's mercy and blessings in times of trial and requesting a successful outcome to the surgery. Our prayers were answered.

After the procedure, the doctor approached me, shook my hand, and said, "Everything went very well. When you visit your wife in recovery, she may be a bit groggy due to the anes-thesia, but she is fine."

> 92
> SOMETIMES, WE FIND OURSELVES IN SITUATIONS BEYOND OUR CONTROL. IT IS IN THOSE HOURS THAT WE MUST PRAY AND TRUST IN GOD

Rachel, Esther's sister, had returned from France the night before and came in the morning to meet us at the hospital to offer support and join us in prayer. She had just arrived when the doctor came out to give me a report on Esther's condition. When the conversation ended, Rachel and I thanked God and the doctor and headed into the recovery room to see Esther.

There was my wife, looking as pretty as ever, though in a slight state of confusion. She could not comprehend the conver-sation well and had little recollection of the accident. A couple of hours later, once Esther was taken upstairs to her room and regained consciousness, the doctor came in to see how she was doing. As we talked, he noticed that I was limping. "What happened?" he asked with a concerned expression."

"My right knee has been giving me trouble, but I trust that God will help me to heal," I replied.

"Why don't you let me take an X-ray when you come in with Esther?" the doctor suggested.

"That's a good idea!" I said, feeling relieved.

> **93**
> DETOURS MAY SEEM FRUSTRATING AT TIMES, BUT THEY OFTEN PROVIDE ROAD SIGNS TO THE APPROPIATE DESTINATION. LET GOD BE YOUR TOUR GUIDE

In the interim, we took time to rest, converse, and pray. When the doctor entered the room, he explained Esther's condition and the outcome of the surgery. He said she would regain eighty percent of her arm's range of motion. However, the extent of her recovery would depend on her diligence with physical therapy. Without physical exercise, she would be more restricted. I again expressed gratitude to the doctor, promising Esther would attend physical therapy.

Esther was released from the hospital, and within a week, we returned to the doctor's office for therapy clearance. I then told the nurse that the doctor wanted to X-ray my knees. A few minutes later, I was called in. After that, both of us proceeded to the examination room. The doctor reiterated his instruction that Esther should engage in physical therapy either next door to the hospital or at a venue of her choosing. Esther agreed and was very happy that the procedure had gone so well. Then, the doctor addressed my X-rays and held them to the light.

"It looks like your right knee bones are rubbing together, and you are a candidate for a replacement," the doctor said.

"Doctor, is there something you can do in the meantime to avoid surgery? I know that God will heal me and provide me with a new knee without an operation," I suggested.

**94
NEVER ALLOW FEAR
TO DICTATE THE DECISIONS
THAT YOU MAKE OR IMPEDE
YOU FROM LISTENING
TO GOD'S WHISPER**

"I can give you a cortisone shot and medication for pain, but the injection will wear out after a few months," he cautioned.

"Let me proceed that way, and I will keep you posted," I replied, grateful for the opportunity to avoid immediate surgery. I thanked and trusted God and firmly believed I was going through this test for a purpose, according to divine planning.

The following morning, I put on the tefillin during prayers and thanked God for protecting and guiding us on the right path. Had it not been for Esther's accident, I would never have become aware of the severity of my knee condition, and most likely, I would have postponed my own medical visit. Therefore, although Esther's fall was unfortunate and painful, the outcome served both of us. During our prayers, we affirmed victory even before it took place.

We went for therapy together, continuously praying and believing God would provide the proper guidance. Esther was healing and had resumed her range of motion just enough to perform daily tasks, such as typing, cooking, and using utensils. In all things, we gave gratitude for divine intervention. A couple of months later, she underwent a follow-up examination and was informed that she was healing well. However, the pain in my knee persisted, and the doctor recommended knee replacement surgery again.

"I am not receiving God's message to proceed with the surgery. Would another cortisone injection be appropriate?" I inquired.

"Yes, since you received your last injection a few months ago, I can give you another; but remember, these types of treat-ments can do more harm than good. Surgery would be the best option."

"I understand, but it's not the right time. I just want to wait and trust God's divine plan," I answered.

To the best of my ability, I took medications, vitamins, ther-apeutic treatments, and ointments while entrusting my recu-peration and healing to the Ultimate Physician. I recalled Aunt Raquel's advice to have faith in God and affirm the victory before its manifestation—as if it already happened. After all, I could not predict who would prescribe the proper treatment or when the healing would take place. It was all in God's hands, destined to occur in Divine time.

Two months passed, and we went on a Caribbean cruise. My pain was intermittent but still prevented me from embarking on foot, and I had to request a wheelchair. All the while, I did not doubt that victory was forthcoming.

Over four years, I tried different healing methods and med-ications and received medical opinions from various doctors. One friend recommended an orthopedic surgeon, and I made an appointment with the doctor, who prescribed a heavy knee brace that did not work for me. Another doctor (Rachel and Sal rec-ommended) suggested a stem cell treatment, which also failed. So, we remained prayerful and decided to return to our original orthopedic doctor.

**95
EVERY LESSON LEARNED –
NO MATTER HOW PAINTFUL –
HAS A DIVINE MEANING
AND PURPOSE**

Once again, the surgery option surfaced and was scheduled for fall 2016. First, however, I had to receive clearance from my primary care doctor within a week. The night before the appoint-ment, I spiked a fever and had chills throughout the evening. The next morning, the primary care physician diagnosed me with a urinary tract infection. As a result, my doctor canceled the knee operation and scheduled me for an appointment with a urologist. When I went for my visit, that specialist informed me that I had a polyp that needed removal and scheduled me

SUCCESS & PROSPERITY

for outpatient surgery in two weeks. He also prescribed a ten-day course of antibiotics to take before the procedure.

Throughout this ordeal, we kept calm and God-centered, focused on divine purpose and our innate conviction that God would provide victory. We knew that there was a good reason behind the apparent setback, and instead of condemning God in times of crisis, we believed that the Creator had a higher purpose for our ultimate benefit.

96
AFFIRM THE VICTORY PRIOR TO ITS MANIFASTATION. DESPITE APPEARANCES. GOD WILL MAKE IT HAPPEN.

Amid everything happening, Sara invited us to an event to celebrate the completion of a course she had taken. We were extremely proud of her and would not let our ailments get in the way of that occasion. We met a friend from our synagogue at the event who inquired about my knee. When I explained my circumstances, our friend said, "I was not going to attend this ceremony, but now I know why I had to be here." Quickly, she wrote down a doctor's name and handed the paper to me. "Call Dr. Barry, specializing in orthopedics, bone manipulation, and alignment, which results in pain relief," she said.

I gratefully took our friend's advice and promised to make the call. After the ceremony, I received word that the urologist had postponed the polyp-removal procedure for January. I saw these occurrences as signs from God that the knee operation would not be necessary—and I was right. Just one appointment with Dr. Barry helped; after two subsequent treatments, the knee felt like new. We praised God for that victory, knowing divine guidance had always been at play. Esther also underwent knee treatment for some pain that had developed, and she felt fine.

After witnessing the victory concerning my knee problems, I decided to cancel the urological procedure, sensing that the right plan was forthcoming, once and ever again, with divine intervention. Two months later, I received a second opinion from another urologist close to home. The moment we saw this doctor, we knew that the presence of God was within him. He told me to return two days later for a more invasive examina-tion to determine whether or not the surgery was necessary. We continued to pray and trusted that God was in control. When the time came, I returned to the doctor with Esther and underwent an examination. The doctor saw that I had only one polyp, which did not appear to be malignant. However, the doctor removed it and sent it to the lab for a biopsy just to be sure. When the results came back negative, we were very relieved and thanked God for the outcome.

97
WHEN YOU TAKE A CHALLENGE AND TURN IT INTO AN EXPRESSION OF LOVE AND GRATITUDE TO THE CREATOR, THE OUTCOME WILL EXCEED YOUR EXPECTATIONS

SUCCESS & PROSPERITY

This is another testimony of how God allowed us to go from a celebration to a test and ultimately to a victory:

On the Memorial Day weekend, the family visited us at our condo, and we spent the day together. Sara kindly volunteered to cook a wholesome organic meal and dessert. Beforehand, we changed into our bathing suits to go for a swim in the pool downstairs. As we headed to the pool, an unexpected event changed our plans for the entire day. Esther fell on the stairs, cut her toe, and hit her bad shoulder, arm, and leg. We were shaken and worried about the fall, but Esther's main concern was her shoulder. As she began to lift herself up, we noticed a lot of blood on the floor. Just then, a resident of the condomin-ium where we resided stopped to assist, like a good angel that came to us out of the blue. He said, "Can I help? I am a doctor. Please let me check to determine the source of the bleeding." He checked Esther's feet, noticed her cut was very deep, and asked the security guard to bring a first-aid kit.

> **98**
> THE FORCES OF GOODNESS AND KINDNESS SURROUND US IN MANY DIFFERENT WAYS. WE MUST ACKNOWLEDGE GOD'S PRESENCE IN TIMES OF DISTRESS, AS WELL AS IN PROSPERITY.

Once he received the necessary aid, the doctor began to dress the wound, all the while reassuring Esther that everything would be fine. After taking care of her, he told us that she had to go to the hospital for X-rays and a tetanus shot. Slowly, as we made our way to the apartment,

Esther declared cheerfully, "Let's eat the delicious food Sara lovingly cooked, and then Mordechai will take me to the hospital." Everyone agreed. Sara and her mother, Janice, served the meal so Esther wouldn't have to put pressure on her injured toe.

After dinner, everyone left, and we went to the hospital. Our neighbor/doctor -friend accurately suggested precautions, and we followed his recommendations. Late into the night, until after midnight, we remained in the hospital, thanking and praising God for sending an angel to protect Esther and take care of us.

Two days later, I experienced a cramp that momentarily paralyzed my arm and back. Thankfully, the episode slowly subsided. Esther observed, "This is a sign telling you that God wants you to take care of that problem." I agreed, and we both went to the doctor, who recommended an MRI of my neck. There we were—Esther with her injured toe and I with my cramp, but throughout our ordeal, we praised and gave glory unto God for testing us.

From then on, we knew, in our hearts, that this was a testimony to carry us through life, always placing faith in divine timing and purpose. Looking back, we realize that everything happens for a reason, and if we don't struggle or become discouraged, hope and promise will always shine upon us.

99
ALL THINGS IN LIFE OCCUR FOR A REASON, AND IF WE DWELL IN THE LIGHT OF HOPE AND PROMISE, GOD WILL SEE US THROUGH

Lessons In Overcoming Challenges and Encountering a Higher Purpose

At times, trouble visits our doorstep and brings uninvited guests. In that instance, a domino effect occurs, in which we are presented with one test after another. In the above circum-stances, our tribulations seemed to pile up, and God was testing our health, but we did not give up. Instead, we concentrated on the ultimate force of goodness that sustains us in all things. We began to meditate and pray and reflect on our past actions.

To share the love of God is not only achieved by giving money to charity. God also wants us to offer words of hope to those who require it, show more compassion to our family and friends, visit the sick, and console those going through difficult trials. We wanted to extend a hand in the Creator's name as if the Divine Source were assisting. As we rectified our actions and allowed God to guide us in the right direction, we observed the Almighty's blessings multiply in our life. Of course, other tests would await us and could not be avoided. We had to learn that God wants to talk to us whenever trials confront us and we are not paying attention.

It is often easier to ask "why" and feel victimized and adrift in an ocean of difficulties and self-pity, nearly drowning without a life raft, but the truth is that we are never alone. Our Supreme Lifeguard will always instruct and protect us if we only become aware and listen. The choices we make are not always ours alone. Sometimes, they are the handiwork of God. Our free will is selective. Therefore, we must understand that we are directed not only by our minds and senses but also by our spirits, have a mission, and are the essence of God that will live forever.

That is why questioning the occurrence of unfortunate or unfavorable circumstances gets us nowhere. Instead, we must reinvest the energy we use in life's "whys" and channel it into gratitude and prayer. When we pray and seek guidance, the answers always surface—even if they do not enter our immediate realm of perception. Often, the answers are long in the making. Remember that anything worth having is worth the wait and the effort.

> **100**
> **FREE WILL IS SELECTIVE. WE ARE NOT ONLY DIRECTED BY OUR MINDS AND SENSES, BUT ALSO BY OUR SPIRIT, WITH THE PURPOSE OF COMPLETING OUR MISSION ON EARTH**

Striving, however, does not mean struggling. Instead, moving in the right direction involves patience, prayerfulness, and inner awareness that God has a plan that must be carried out. That is the reason why there are no coincidences. The postponement of the inevitable—God's plan—sometimes appears to be an obstacle, but it is a blessing waiting to happen (e.g., the post-ponement of my procedures).

In every case, the best action is to trust in God and allow the Creator to influence our intuition. We must have patience and allow life to flow according to divine will instead of human in-tervention. When we let go and allow God to guide us in taking the wheel and veering us in the right direction, the best results follow. Human beings tend to believe that we have the power to facilitate and effectuate outcomes—and to a large extent, we do—but not without God's hand in envisioning a positive result. Assuming the power alone gives us the false perception that we are in control, but if we attempt to accomplish things alone, we inevitably become disillusioned.

SUCCESS & PROSPERITY

Every test has a purpose, and every trial and tribulation has a meaning. So, the next time we find ourselves in a crisis, the best and most permanent solution is to call upon the Great Architect of our lives and humbly request guidance and advice. If we listen, the answers never fail to appear. Life is filled with surprises, all predetermined by God-mind, which holds sway over all of us.

It is important to remember that no matter what kinds of tests and tribulations we go through, we must ask God to provide us with opportunities to perform acts of love, kindness, and charity. In doing so, we will find that when we shift our focus from ourselves to others in pain, our challenges and sorrows diminish, and we are filled with joy derived from helping and caring for other human beings.

**101
IT IS IMPORTANT THAT
WE ASK GOD FOR OPPORTUNITIES
TO PERFORM ACTS OF LOVE AND KINDNESS
IN THE MIDST OF OUR
TESTS AND TRIBULATIONS**

CHAPTER 10

THE LOVE OF GOD INSPIRES US TO LOVE OTHERS

To achieve success in this world and complete the mission that God has given us, we must practice one of the most important aspects of that mission: Loving our families and friends as we love ourselves—and as God loves us. Each one of us is a unique creation unto ourselves. God has allowed us to incarnate into our bodies and has given us definitive missions in the world so that we can grow in spirit. Each day, it is essential for us to maintain the proper attitudes and perspectives in our lives. We cannot allow circumstances to determine the outcome. Everything that happens in our daily lives is a test for us to learn and enhance our skills in our careers and physical activities, improve our health, family relationships, and similar issues we encounter on the journey.

When we love and respect ourselves, we understand our purpose while accepting the challenges we face along the way, secure in the knowledge that God will grant us victories, no matter how difficult our hardships may be. As we move through obstacles, we realize that God has a purpose for placing them in our path, and there are lessons to be learned from them. We must let God help us transform our tests and tribulations into victories that we can utilize as testimonials to help others in similar circumstances.

When speaking of loving ourselves, we do not mean brag-gadocio, narcissism, or excessive self-indulgence. True spiritual love is humility and confidence in our abilities, understanding that we are comprised of body and spirit. The body is a temporary vehicle that the soul needs to achieve its mission, to go toward the fulfillment of our life's mission, realizing—at every step of the way—that there are other journeys in progress, as well.

Genuine self-love enables us to confer and receive love, in turn, and to be instruments of God's loving force and guidance. Our compassionate intervention in others' lives can change how others view their problems and embolden them to confront their own challenges and tests. No one is immune to life's constant ups and downs, and we all need each other. Acknowledging that everyone's mission has value and may be intertwined with others is essential in helping people and simultaneously evolving as human beings.

This is true of the family ecosystem. One of the most critical parts of our mission in this world is to be able to assist family members with the love, knowledge, and financial support that God provides us. We must not shy away from that mission. God's reason for placing us in particular families is to allow us to be of service to a small circle of close individuals before branching out to assist others at large. In some instances, we view the grass to be greener on the other side of the fence, and we avoid our responsibilities to those nearest and dearest for the sake of being in the company of others or receiving other sources of validation. In these cases, we are being misguided by our limited human minds instead of paying heed to the eternal God-mind that directs the course of every life. Often, we also pay attention to materialistic influences that lead us nowhere.

102
WE MUST LOVE ONE ANOTHER AS WE LOVE OURSELVES AND ACKNOWLEDGE THAT WE ARE PART OF THE HUMAN FAMILY

Even in situations where, when we are children, we endure ridicule, insults, and bullying, if the Master of the Universe has placed us in those circumstances to test our faith, the Creator wants to witness our degree of determination and ability to withstand adversity. God wants us to be strong and prepare for spiritual and material advancement. We should never be deflected from our goals or discouraged by the judgment of others, for it is through God's love and wisdom that we are who we are. We are God's creation, we came through our parents, but we originally emanated from the Creator. We have been placed here on earth according to God's direction with a mission. Others' negative options are irrelevant, therefore. We must un-derstand that we are descendants of God, our Creator, and our human family circle is integral to our mission to depurate our soul. Therefore, in our daily lives, we must do the following:

> *We must sow love when hate exists:*
> *Engage in acts of kindness instead of vindictiveness or revenge;*
> *Understand instead of being understood;*
> *Forgive—even when we know, deep in our hearts, that we have not transgressed but, rather, others have wronged us.*

In other words, we must love unconditionally and emulate God's love among our family, friends, and acquaintances. Looking around us, we observe challenges to overcome in our family and everyone surrounding us. This is true even if, on the surface, some families appear content and well-adjust-ed. One issue or another always threatens to upset or disrupt families. Sometimes, these problems may appear to be unbear-able. However, with God, all things are possible, and any intra-family discord we may face is also happening for a purpose. The tests we endure increase our patience and love and enhance our capacity for demonstrating great compassion for others. As human beings, our typical reaction to problems at home, with our mates, at work, and school is to escape the difficul-ties by either physically removing ourselves from the challeng-ing environment, divorcing our spouse, moving away from our families, quitting our jobs, or changing classes or schools. In so acting, we hurt ourselves and others. We are in the world to prosper spiritually and materially by overcoming the challenges God presents to us in our Circle of Life. When we turn what is negative and painful into testimonies of faith, love, and com-passion for others, we will watch ourselves go from victory to victory.

When we love others as we love ourselves, we understand that we all experience similar trials and hardships and share many of the same dreams and goals—the desire for love, understanding, compassion, security, etc. Planet Earth is enormous, and there is room for all kinds of individuals, ideologies, and practices. It is important to acknowledge that every belief system has its place in the Grand Scheme as long as it operates on ethical, trust-worthy, and loving principles. Those individuals who seek to exclude others because they have different perspectives, faiths, or practices attempt to close off whole segments of the popula-tion that are simply trying to fulfill their missions according to the dictates of a benevolent, loving God—the parent of our human family—the ultimate Source and Creator.

103
TRUE SELF-LOVE IS SPIRITUAL LOVE THAT GUIDES US TO BECOMING HUMBLE AND CONFIDENT IN OUR ABILITIES

We were born into the family we chose to complete our mission at God's direction. Once we incarnate into a newborn, we forget everything from the previous life and all the teachings that God provided to our spirit while incarnating in a new body. As we grow, we often take our families for granted. We must remember that our nuclear family is the foundation and corner-stone of our lives, which enhances our chances of making the right choice regarding our soulmates. The divinely inspired op-portunity to choose our life partners and create our Circle of Love within the world at large allows us to experience God's love and compassion. Divine recognition, in turn, helps us to grow.

SUCCESS & PROSPERITY

104
UNCONDITIONAL LOVE, FAITH, AND TRUST IN GOD ARE THE FOUNDATIONAL PRINCIPLES FOR LIVING A SUCCESSFUL LIFE.

Sometimes, friends or co-workers become like family and are our "chosen" relatives. In whatever ways we form our family, loving them as we love ourselves and as God loves us ensures continuity and the ever-present blessings of compassion and harmony within that intimate circle.

Unconditionally loving one another opens many possibili-ties for forming lasting relationships—on every level. It helps us to achieve success in business, career, family, health, peace, and happiness as we grow spiritually—all through faith and trusting God in everything.

Amen.

105
LOVE IS THE ANSWER. WE MUST LOVE GOD AND OTHERS AS WE LOVE OURSELVES

CONCLUDING THOUGHTS FROM "MR. AMEN"

Whenever my spirit soars, I always affirm, "Amen!" to emphasize my endorsement of the sentiment or pronouncement that someone—a friend, a family member, our rabbi, etc.—puts forth, whether the message is spiritual or a positive affirmation. I love to offer support, affir-mations, and encouragement by saying, "AMEN!" The habit was embedded within me from an early age, and I always recommend that others exclaim "AMEN!" whenever they want to endorse a particular phrase or form of a positive or spiritual expression. When we say "Amen!" we receive the entire blessing as if we had said it ourselves. As I approached my seventieth birthday, my heart was filled with the divinely inspired desire to write this book, despite our limited academic training. My wife and I felt confident and placed our faith in God to present us with the right person who could assist us in accomplishing our goal, and we believed that we had already fulfilled our objective.

We truly believe that faith in God is the belief in things to come in the future as if there were happening now. We must repeatedly present our prayers and wishes before God as if they were being answered now and persevere until God grants what is best for us. If you, our readers, take away only one message from this book, try to practice faith in God every day for twenty-one days, and you will see the difference in your life.

Our thoughts merit summarizing here to bring out our core message—a straightforward concept that will hopefully provide our readers with the understanding of how to live a successful life through faith in God. Understanding the art of persistence and perseverance, living in gratitude, performing acts of love and kindness, acknowledging the importance of repentance for our mistakes, accepting everyone as equal, learning to yield our will to our spirit, and not allowing our earthly inclinations to influence our decisions—this is the path to success. Of course, we must make sure that we ask God for guidance every day before making decisions. All these are essential ingredients for living a life of abundance, prosperity, happiness, and peace in every phase of life.

All of us are born with a specific mission, which we must fulfill throughout our lives. During the evolution of our lives, we encounter joys and sorrows, sunshine and storms, which all serve as tests of our resilience and patience to withstand our trials, correct our mistakes from our past and present incarna-tions, and provide us with a chance to grow in faith and glorify our Creator. We must never ask "why," as God has a time and purpose for everything—all for our benefit. Belief in our Divine Source will grant us victory, no matter what is happening in our lives. We must maintain our faith in God and have patience to wait for God's time.

It has been said that, at the moment of birth, an angel touches our upper lips to allow our spirits to forget our past lives, and the teachings that the angels administered to us, so that we could begin from scratch so that we can learn to love our family, have faith in God, and understand the importance of serving others, all while achieving our mission and acquiring success on earth and in the world to come.

During our earthly pilgrimage, humans encounter angels repeatedly to guide and uplift us. Angels are not only ethereal beings with wings but often appear in human form to teach us a lesson and offer protection and words of encouragement that change our perspectives.

Our Circle of Love enhances our journey in the physical world—our nuclear family (comprised of our parents, siblings, aunts, uncles, and other relatives), and that circle expands when we choose to marry. Finding one's soulmate is a crucial step in our spiritual, emotional, and psychological development and occurs when two hearts unite with common goals and dreams and become one pillar of strength. When couples form their own family, separate ideological perspectives must merge through compromise and understanding.

In every relationship and dealings with others—whether at home, work, school, or other surroundings, acts, and words of love and kindness, compliments and affirmations of goodwill serve to encourage other people to do the same. Every human being can become part of God's Angelic Army just by forming the intention to serve and emulate our Creator and perpetu-ate love and goodwill wherever we go. In this way, we are God's servants and agents of protection and thereby accumu-late our "spiritual income." Correspondingly, we decrease our emotional and spiritual deficit. We must meditate, analyze, and monitor our spiritual and material revenues. If we do not change our mindsets to correct and improve how we conduct our lives today but continue to expect different results, we will proceed irrationally and give in to the correct definition of "insanity." Everything we do is a process, and to achieve positive results, we must apply all these principles—or perhaps others that produce the desired results and God's intended blessings. Our excuses for not succeeding are merely rationalizations for our failures.

Balance is of utmost importance in life, but most significant of all is our ability to love and be loved and to generate feelings of security and happiness for others and ourselves. This love must be unconditional, perpetual, and everlasting, regardless of self-gain and interest.

When we give of our hearts without expectation, we exhibit the true essence of God and the Creator's purpose for us on earth. Then, with surrender, everything occurs in Divine Time, according to Supreme Will. Understanding and practicing these concepts enables us to live a life of fulfillment, blessings, and success.

It is our wish and prayer that God will grant you all you desire and success in all you strive to achieve.

AMEN!

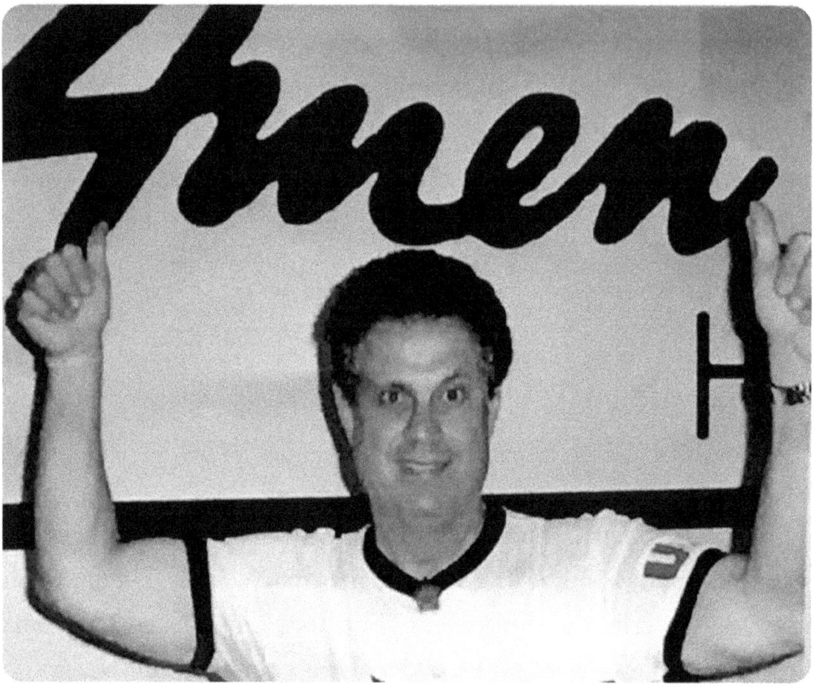

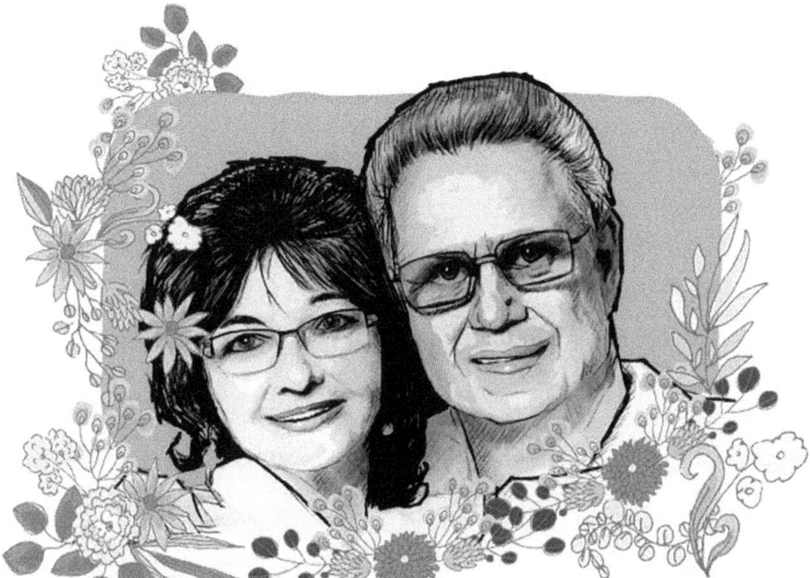

The following list of quotations is a reference for the flower-framed quotes in each chapter of this text.

LIST OF QUOTATIONS

1—THE ENERGY OF OUR SOUL DOES NOT HAVE A COLOR OR A GENDER. IT IS PART OF THE ENERGY OF GOD (PAGE 1)

2—WE MUST THINK OF FAITH IN GOD AS THE COMMON THREAD THAT UNIFIES ALL OF US (PAGE 2)

3—IF YOU BELIEVE, ALL THINGS ARE POSSIBLE. IT ALL STARTS BY INVITING GOD INTO YOUR LIFE (PAGE 3)

4—MY TRUST AND CONCENTRATION IS ALWAYS FOCUSED ON GOD, THE PROVIDER OF ALL THINGS. (PAGE 5)

5—GOD ALLOWS STUMBLING BLOCKS AND NEGATIVE PEOPLE TO TEST AND PROVIDE US WITH THE TOOLS OF FAITH TO HAVE VICTORY AND MOVE US TO THE NEXT LEVEL (PAGE 7)

6—GOD PROVIDES THE VICTORY TO THOSE WHO PATIENTLY WAIT FOR DIVINE MERCY WHILE STRIVING TOWARD THEIR GOAL (PAGE 9)

7—GOD IS THE PROVIDER OF EVERYTHING. GOD WILL BE WITH ME ALL THE DAYS OF MY LIFE. I WILL TRY MY BEST, WITH PERSISTENCE AND FAITH, AND GOD WILL DO THE REST (PAGE 11)

8—GOD IS ALWAYS WORKING FOR OUR BENEFIT, EVEN IN THE MIDST OF THE GREATEST TRIALS (PAGE 12)

9—FAITH IS THE BELIEF THAT GOD IS IN CONTROL – AND WHATEVER HAPPENS IS FOR THE BEST (PAGE 13)

10—WHEN DESTINY IS BEFORE YOU, SAY WHAT YOU NEED TO SAY. DO NOT HOLD BACK (PAGE 21)

11—SPOKEN WORDS OF WISDOM ARE THE ECHOES OF GOD'S VOICE (PAGE 22)

12—GOD'S HAND IS IN THE DETAILS. SOMETIMES, IT MANIFESTS THROUGH THE TEACHING AND GUIDANCE OF OTHERS (PAGE 23).

13—PERSISTENCE, WHEN COUPLED WITH FAITH, IS THE MOST IMPORTANT FACTOR WHEN YOU ARE SEARCHING FOR A SOULMATE (PAGE 24)

14—GOD ORCHESTRATES THE UNION OF SOULS. IT IS UP TO US TO FOLLOW THROUGH (PAGE 25)

15—BE PATIENT. GOD HAS A PLAN. YOU JUST HAVE TO KEEP BELIEVING (PAGE 27).

16—WHEN IT RAINS, SOMETIMES GOD IS POURING DOWN LOVE. WATCH FOR GOD'S SIGNS (PAGE 28)

17—DO NOT LET LOVE BE AN EXCUSE TO RELIEVE YOU FROM YOUR OBLIGATIONS (PAGE 29)

18—LOVE INVOLVES SACRIFICES, BUT THE GIVE-AND-TKE IS PART OF GOD'S TEST OF TRUE LOVE (PAGE 31)

19—WHEN WE BELIEVE, GOD ALWAYS PROVIDES (PAGE 32)

20—GOD ALWAYS PUTS THE RIGHT PEOPLE IN THE PATH OF THOSE WHO SEEK DIVINE GUIDANCE (PAGE 33)

21—NEVER HEED THE VOICES OF DOUBT AND NEGATIVITY . INSTEAD, PLACE YOUR FAITH IN GOD AND BE (PAGE 34)

22—CREATING OUR OWN CIRCLE OF LOVE IS PART OF SPIRITUAL GROWTH (PAGE 42)

23—OUR SEARCH FOR OUR SOULMATE STARTS AS EARLY AS OUR YOUNG ADULTHOOD (PAGE 43)

24—SOULMATES SHOULD NOT BE CHOSEN BASED ON PHYSICAL ATTRACTION ALONE, BUT INSTEAD, ON THE SPIRITUAL V ALUES AND BELIEFS THA T WILL HELP THE COUPLE TO BE BETTER PEOPLE AND ATTAIN HAPPINESS IN THIS WORLD AND IN THE WORLD TO COME (PAGE 44)

25—WHEN CHOOSING A SOULMATE, RELY ON YOUR INNER VOICE AND YOUR INTUITIVE SENSES, AND IGNORE EXTERNAL NEGATIVITY AND DOUBT (PAGE 45)

26—IN TIMES OF CRISIS —AS AT ALL TIMES— SHARE IDEAS WITH YOUR SOULMATE WITH LOVE AND RESPECT, AND ALLOW GOD TO ACT AS YOUR COMPASS (PAGE 47)

27—TO SUCCEED IN OUR RELATIONSHIPS, WE CANNOT BE CLOSE-MINDED BUT, RATHER, WE MUST WORK TOGETHER AND HELP EACH OTHER. WE WILL THEN FEEL THE PRESENCE OF GOD'S BLESSINGS (PAGE 48)

28—OPEN COMMUNICATION, HONESTY, AND WILLINGNESS TO CULTIVATE MUTUALLY SHARED VALUES AND DREAMS ARE THE HALLMARKS OF A GREAT AND LASTING PARTNERSHIP (PAGE 49)

29—TO AVOID UNNECESSARY CONFLICTS, DISCUSS YOUR BELIEFS AND PREFERENCES OPENLY WITH YOUR SOULMATE TO FORMULATE YOUR OWN RULES WITHIN THE MARRIAGE (PAGE 50)

30—TO A VOID PERSONAL CONFLICTS. RELIGIOUS EDUCATION, AND PRACTICES SHOULD BE AGREED UPON BEFORE THE CHILDREN ARE BORN (PAGE 51)

31—RIDE OUT THE STORM TOGETHER AS A COUPLE AND DON'T ALLOCATE BLAME TO OTHERS FOR ANY DIFFICULTIES THAT MAY ARISE. SEE EACH OTHER THROUGH TO VICTORY (PAGE 52)

32—RELEASE ANY DISCORD THAT YOU MAY FEEL TOWARD ONE ANOTHER AS A COUPLE, AND NEVER GO TO SLEEP ANGRY. KISS AND MAKE UP (PAGE 54)

33—MUTUAL RESPECT AND APPROPIATE LANGUAGE SHOULD ALWAYS BEUSED IN FRONT OF THE CHILDREN, FAMILY AND FRIENDS (PAGE 55)

34—CONFLICTS OF OPINION SHOULD NOT CAUSE ARGUMENTATION. ALWAYS TRY TO REACH A COMPROMISE (PAGE 57)

35—PRACTICE TOLERANCE, PATIENCE, AND MUTUAL UNDERSTANDING TO CREATE A HARMONIOUS AND PEACEFULHOMELIFE. (PAGE 58)

36—COUPLES SHOULD MAKE FINANCIAL DECISIONS AS ONE ENTITY, WITHOUT BEING SWAYED BY OUTSIDE INFLUENCES (PAGE 60)

37—MAKE DECISIONS IN A TRIANGLE: GOD, YOU, AND YOUR PARTNER (PAGE 61)

38—EXPRESSIONS OF LOVE ARE NOT JUST PHYSICAL. INTIMACY SHOULD BE SPONTANEOUS AND FROM THE HEART (PAGE 63)

39—A COUPLE'S LOVE FOR EACH OTHER SHOULD BE A LIVING TESTAMENT TO GOD'S BLESSINGS (PAGE 63)

40—LOVING MEMORIES ARE THE LIGHTS THAT SPARKS THE FLAME OF LOVE (PAGE 65)

41—SIGNS OF COMMITMENT AND LOVE GROW SIGNIFICANTLY THROUGHOUT THE YEARS. HONOR YOUR VOWS BY CREATING LASTING MEMORIES (PAGE 66)

42— BY TRUSTING IN GOD. WE WILL ACHIEVE BALANCE AND ALLOW BLESSINGS AND PEACE TO FOLLOW (PAGE 67)

43—BELIEVERS AND NON-BELIEVERS CAN CO-EXIST IN THE WORLD. WE ARE ALL ON THIS JOURNEY TOGETHER (PAGE 72)

44—BESTOW FAITH WHERE THERE IS DOUBT, BESTOW LOVE WHERE HATE IS PRESENT, BESTOW UNDERSTANDING WHERE THERE IS INDIFFERENCE, BESTOW ACCEPTANCE WHERE THERE IS REJECTION,

BESTOW PARDON WHERE THERE ARE CONFLICTS, BESTOW BLESSINGS WHERE THERE ARE CURSES (PAGE 73)

45—BE A FORCE FOR GOOD IN THE WORLD TO COUNTERACT FORCES OF EVIL, NEGATIVITYAND INDIFERENCE (PAGE 78)

46—ALLOW GOD TO BE YOUR ETERNAL GUIDING COMPASS THAT LEADS YOU TO THE FULFILLMENT OF YOUR MISSION (PAGE 79)

47—GOD HAS A PURPOSE AND A REASON FOR EVERYTHING. TESTS ARE THE BUILDING BLOCKS OF VICTORY (PAGE 80)

48—CHOOSING TO DO THINGS GOD'S WAY MEANS CONSCIOUSLY SURRENDERING TO A GREATER WISDOM THAN OUR LIMITED HUMAN UNDERSTANDING (PAGE 81)

49—WHEN WE ARE PRESENT AND IN TUNE WITH THE CREATOR, WE KNOW THAT WE ARE "DOING IT GOD'S WAY (PAGE 83)

50—STRUCTURING OUR LIVES AROUND GRATITUDE TO GOD SHOWS US THE PATH TO ABUNDANCE (PAGE 84)

51—EVERY TIME YOU GIVE WITH HONORABLE INTENTION, YOU RECEIVE MUCH MORE BECAUSE YOU ARE DOING GOD'S WILL (PAGE 85)

52—WE ARE ALL PART OF AN INTERCONNECTED CHAIN OF HUMANITY. IT IS IMPORTANT TO CHEER AND

UPLIFT OTHERS —ALL TO THE GLORY OF GOD (PAGE 86)

53—HAVE PATIENCE AND TRUST IN DIVINE TIMING, WHICH IS INFINITE, RATHER THAN VIEWING LIFE FROM OUR LIMITED PERSPECTIVE (PAGE 88)

54—WE CAN OBTAIN EVERYTHING THAT WE DESIRE AS LONG AS WE DO IT GOD'S WAY, HAVE PATIENCE, AND REST ON GOD'S TIME (PAGE 88)

55—KINDNESS IS INFECTOUS. THE MORE WE GIVE, THE MORE WE RECEIVE. AS A RESULT, WE WITNESS THE FRUITS OF OUR GIVING REFLECTED IN THE WORLD AROUND US, MANIFESTING A TRUE REPRESENTATION OF GOD (PAGE 90)

56—WALKING THE ROAD GOD'S WAY ALSO REMINDS US OF THE MOST IMPORTANT REASON FOR OUR EXISTENCE:TO FULFILL OUR SPIRITUAL MISSION (PAGE 91)

57—CONSULTATION WITH GOD IS THE FIRST CRITICAL STEP IN THE DECISION-MAKING PROCESS (PAGE 92)

58—JOINT DECISION-MAKING AND MUTUAL ACCORD ARE ESSENTIAL IN EVERY MARRIAGE (PAGE 94)

59—GOD WILL USE THE OUTCOME OF OUR DECISIONS TO DEMOSTRATE THAT THERE IS A DIVINE PURPOSE IN EVERY ASPECT OF OUR LIVES (PAGE 97)

60—WHAT WE DO IN THIS LIFE WILL ULTIMATELY AFFECT OUR ETERNAL LIVES (PAGE 99)

61—AT TIMES, HUMANS REQUIRE A BIT OF NUDGING AND INSPIRATION THAT COMES TO US IN THE FORM OF ANGELS (PAGE 100)

62—NOT EVERYTHING GOES RIGHT ALL THE TIME. WHEN THINGS DO NOT TURN OUT ACCORDING TO OUR EXPECTATIONS, WE HAVE COMPLETE FAITH THAT EVERYTHING WILL WORK FOR THE BEST (PAGE 102)

63—WHEN YOU LEAST EXPECT IT, GOD SENDS ANGELS TO PROVIDE YOU WITH A TESTIMONY OF FAITH (PAGE 103)

64—" B' SHEM HASHEM NAAHASE V' NESLIACH" "IN THE NAME OF GOD, IT WILL BE DONE, AND YOU WILL SUCCEED" (PAGE 104)

65—WHEN WE LIVE BY FAITH, GOD PROVIDES US WITH THE VICTORY (PAGE 105)

66—ANGELS NEED NOT HAVE WINGS TO BE MESSENGERS OF GOD. THEY CAN APPEAR IN ALL SORTS OF WAYS AND IN THE LEAST EXPECTED PLACES (PAGE 106).

67—ANGELS CONFIRM GOD'S TRUTH THAT WE HARBOR INSIDE, BUT SOMETIMES IGNORE OR FAIL TO ACKNOWLEDGE (PAGE 108)

68—WE CAN ALL BE PART OF GOD'S ANGELIC ARMY BY HELPING OTHERS AND SPREADING WORDS AND ACTS OF LOVE AND KINDNESS (PAGE 109)

69—SSEEK AND ACT UPON OPPORTUNITIES TO BECOME GOD'S SPIRITUAL AGENTS (PAGE 110)

70—QUESTIONING WHY IS THE BIGGEST FORM OF REBELLION, AND BLOCKS OUT THE POSSIBILITY OF HAVING FAITH IN GOD (PAGE 118)

71—DOUBT AND FEAR LEAD TO PERPETUAL STRUGGLE AND CONFUSION. DWELLING IN FAITH IN GOD YIELDS ACCEPTANCE AND A CLEAR VISION (PAGE 120)

72—EVERY CHALLENGE IS A LESSON FOR FUTURE TESTS THAT WILL BECOME TESTIMONIES OF FAITH THROUGH BELIEF IN GOD (PAGE 122)

73—GRIEVING FOR THE DEPARTURE OF OUR LOVE ONE IS ALSO AN OPPORTUNITY TO REFLECT ON THEIR –AND OUR —CONTRIBUTIONS TO THE WORLD (PAGE 123)

74—EVERYONE HAS A TIME AND A PURPOSE TO COMPLETE THEIR MISSION ACCORDING TO GOD'S WILL (PAGE 124)

75—WE CALL TODAY "THE PRESENT" BECAUSE IT IS THE GIFT THAT GOD GIVES US EACH DAY (PAGE 126)

76—SINCE THE BEGINNING OF THE WORLD, GOD HAS MADE KNOWN TO HUMANKIND THE COMMANDS THAT WE MUST FOLLOW ON EARTH TO LIVE PEACEFULLY AND RECEIVE ETERNAL LIFE (PAGE 127)

77—WE CANNOT EXPECT TO UNDERSTAND GOD'S PLAN ENTIRELY UNTIL OUR MISSION IS COMPLETED. THEREFORE, TRUST IN THE CREATOR, BE THANKFUL, AND DO WHAT IS BEST IN THE EYES OF GOD (PAGE 128)

78—WE ARE SOULS INCARNATED WITH VARIOUS MISSIONS AND LESSONS TO LEARN ALONG THE WAY (PAGE 129)

79—THE LOVE THAT WE SHARE IS A GIFT THAT GOD WANTS US TO SPREAD TO EVERYONE IN THE WORLD (PAGE 130)

80—FOCUS ON THE MISSION, NOT THE "WHYS" AND THE STRUGGLES. IN SO DOING, MAINTAINING FAITH IN GOD MUST BE SUPREME (PAGE 132)

81—WHEN YOU CONVERT YOUR "WHYS" INTO TRUSTING GOD THROUGH FAITH, YOUR LIFE CHANGES AND GOD GRANTS YOU VICTORIES (PAGE 133)

82—PRAY TO STAY IN FAITH. GOD WILL GUIDE YOUR STEPS, AND YOU WILL NOT HAVE ANY MORE FEAR OR DOUBT (PAGE 134)

83—EMBRACE AND ACKNOWLEDGE GOD'S SHIELD OF PROTECTION AROUND YOU (PAGE 138)

84—RECOGNIZE THE SPIRIT OF DISCERNMENT AND PUT ITS POWER INTO PRACTICE (PAGE 139).

85— DO NOT FEAR THE FORCES OF EVIL. HAVE FAITH AND GOD'S ANGELIC ARMY IS ALWAYS READY TO HELP YOU (PAGE 141)

86—GOD ACTS AS OUR INSTRUCTOR IN THE CLASSROOM OF LIFE (PAGE 142)

87—GOD ACTS LIKE A PARENT, TEACHER OR COACH, WHO ALLOWS US TO UNDERSTAND THE LESSONS IN OUR TESTS (PAGE 143)

88—WALK IN FAITH, AND YOU WILL ULTIMATELY WALK INTO VICTORY (PAGE 144)

89—PRAY TO GOD FOR GUIDANCE AND GOD WILL HELP YOU TO TRANSFORM YOUR LIFE (PAGE 147)

90—NEVER ALLOW YOUR FAITH TO WAVER IN MOMENTS OF CRISIS. THAT IS THE TIME WHEN YOU NEED IT THE MOST (PAGE 148)

91—BEAR SUFFERING WITH PATIENCE, KNOWING THAT THE OUTCOME IS IN GOD'S HANDS –WITH A PURPOSE (PAGE 150)

92—SOMETIMES, WE FIND OURSELVES IN SITUATIONS BEYOND OUR CONTROL. IT IS IN THOSE HOURS THAT WE MUST PRAY AND TRUST IN GOD (PAGE 151)

93—DETOURS MAY SEEM FRUSTRATING AT TIMES, BUT THEY OFTEN PROVIDE ROAD SIGNS TO THE APPROPRIATE DESTINATION. LET GOD BE YOUR TOUR GUIDE (PAGE 152)

94—NEVER ALLOW FEAR TO DICTATE THE DECISIONS THAT YOU MAKE OR IMPEDE YOU FROM LISTENING TO GOD'S WHISPER (PAGE 153)

95—EVERY LESSON LEARNED—NO MATTER HOW PAINTFUL —HAS A DIVINE MEANING AND PURPOSE (PAGE 155)

SUCCESS & PROSPERITY

96—AFFIRM THE VICTORY PRIOR TO ITS MANIFASTATION DESPITE APPEARANCES, AND GOD WILL MAKE IT HAPPEN (PAGE 156)

97—WHEN YOU TAKE A CHALLENGE AND TURN IT INTO AN EXPRESSION OF LOVE AND GRATITUDE TO THE CREATOR, THE OUTCOME WILL EXCEED YOUR EXPECTATIONS (PAGE 157)

98—THE FORCES OF GOODNESS AND KINDNESS SURROUND US IN MANY DIFFERENT WAYS. WE MUST ACKNOWLEDGE GOD'S PRESENCE IN TIMES OF DISTRESS (PAGE 158)

99—ALL THINGS IN LIFE OCCUR FOR A REASON, AND IF WE DWELL IN THE LIGHT OF HOPE AND PROMISE, GOD WILL SEE US THROUGH (PAGE 159)

100—FREE WILL IS SELECTIVE. WE ARE NOT ONLY DIRECTED BY OUR MINDS AND SENSES, BUT ALSO BY OUR SPIRIT, WITH THE PURPOSE OF COMPLETING OUR MISSION ON EARTH (PAGE 161)

101—IT IS IMPORTANT THAT WE ASK GOD FOR OPPORTUNITIES TO PERFORM ACTS OF LOVE AND KINDNESS IN THE MIDST OF OUR TESTS AND TRIBULATIONS (PAGE 162)

102—WE MUST LOVE ONE ANOTHER AS WE LOVE OURSELVES AND ACKNOWLEDGE THAT WE ARE PART OF THE HUMAN FAMILY (PAGE 165)

103—TRUE SELF-LOVE IS SPIRITUAL LOVE THAT GUIDES US TO BECOMING HUMBLE AND CONFIDENT IN OUR ABILITIES (PAGE 167)

104—UNCONDITIONAL LOVE, FAITH AND TRUST IN GOD ARE THE FOUNDATIONAL PRINCIPLES FOR LIVING A SUCCESSFUL LIFE (PAGE 168)

105—LOVE IS THE ANSWER . WE MUST LOVE GOD AND OTHERS AS WE LOVE OURSELVES (PAGE 168)

WE WELCOME FEEDBACK FROM OUR READERS AND INVITE YOU TO VISIT OUR SOCIAL MEDIA PAGES AND WEBSITE.

Visit Our Social Media Pages and Website

Scan the QR Codes

Follow us on

INSTAGRAM:

FACEBOOK:

YOUTUBE:

WEBSITE:

MAKELIFEASUCCESS.COM

Milton Keynes UK
Ingram Content Group UK Ltd.
UKHW041327301124
451950UK00005B/36